ABORTION WITHOUT APOLOGY

A Radical History for the 1990s

by Ninia Baehr

South End Press pamphlet No. 8

•A15043 946731

ILLUSTRATION CREDITS
Most of the illustrations in this pamphlet come from the early abortion movement or from the "second wave of feminism." While some of the artists are unknown, what follows is as complete acknowledgments as was possible. Thanks to all who helped create and collect these graphics.

The graphics on pages 3, 7, and 45 are by Pat McGinnis and are used with her permission.

Page 5: artist unknown; graphic reprinted from *The New Woman's Survival Catalog,* ed. Kirsten Grimstad and Susan Rennie, (New York: Coward McCann and Geoghegan, 1973). It was reprinted there from the cover of *Sister,* July 1973.

Page 23: photographer unknown; reprinted from "How to do Self Examination Using the Plastic Speculum," a flier distributed by the Feminist Women's Health Center, Hollywood, CA, 1972.

Page 24: Suzanne Gage; from Menstrual Extraction brochure reprinted from *Quest* vol. 4, no. 3, summer, 1978, and distributed by Feminist Women's Health Centers.

Page 25: Wen-ti Tsen; the graphic is reprinted from Community Press Features, it originally appeared in *Science for the People,* and is used with the artist's permission.

Page 32: artist is unknown; from *Come Unity* and Community Press Features.

Page 37: Bülbül, Arachne Publishing, P.O. Box 4100, Mountain View, CA 94040; reproduced from *The Monthly Extract: An Irregular Periodical,* January 1978, and May/June 1976; used with the artist's permission.

Page 41: Irene Peslikis; with the artist's permission.

Page 54: artist is unknown; from Community Press Features.

Page 57: artist is unknown; reprinted from *Women Under Attack,* by the CARASA collective (South End Press, 1989).

Page 59: Teresa Flavin; the graphic originally appeared in *Zeta Magazine* and is used with the artist's permission.

Copyright © 1990 by Ninia Baehr
Any properly footnoted quotation of up to 500 sequential words may be used without permission, as long as the total number of words quoted does not exceed 2,000. For longer quotations or for a greater number of words quoted, written permission from the publisher is required.

First edition. Cover design by Ty de Pass. Production by the South End Press collective. Manufactured in the United States.

South End Press, 116 St. Botolph Street, Boston, MA 02115.
99 98 97 96 95 94 93 92 91 90   1 2 3 4 5 6 7 8 9

Library of Congress Cataloging-in-Publication Data
Baehr, Ninia.
Abortion without apology: radical history for the 1990s / Ninia Baehr.
p. cm.
Includes bibliographical references.
ISBN 0-89608-384-5
1. Pro-choice movement—United States. 2. Abortion—Moral and ethical aspects. I. Title.
HQ767.5.U5B34 1990
363.4'6'0973—dc20   90-33244

TABLE OF CONTENTS

Introduction/1

1: The Army of Three:
Making Abortion Public/7

2: Woman-Controlled Abortion:
The Self-Help Health Movement/21

3: Speak Truth to Power:
The New York Fight/31

4: Lessons for the 1990s/51

5: Organizing for the Future/61

Resources/63

Bibliography/65

ACKNOWLEDGMENTS

Abortion Without Apology is based on audiotaped, videotaped, and filmed interviews produced for the "Abortion Rap" workshops and for the film documentary "With a Vengeance," and on letters solicited for this pamphlet. If not otherwise indicated, all quotes are drawn from the following sources:
  Byllye Avery, "In Defense of *Roe*" conference, videotaped April 8, 1989.
  Lucinda Cisler, interview videotaped February 16, 1988.
  Lana Clarke Phelan, interview videotaped November 6, 1987.
  Constance Cook, interview audiotaped February 3, 1987.
  Carol Downer, interview videotaped November 4, 1987.
  Rowena Gurner, interview audiotaped November 5, 1987, and letters dated
    December 13, 1989, and December 15, 1989.
  Brenda Joyner, interview filmed April 8, 1989.
  "Jane," interview filmed November 13, 1988.
  Patricia Maginnis, interview videotaped November 5, 1987, and letter dated
    December 28, 1989.
  Sojourner McCauley, interview filmed June 29, 1989.
  Irene Peslikis, interview audiotaped December 17, 1987, and interview
    videotaped July 14, 1988.
  Lorraine Rothman, interview videotaped November 4, 1987.

Thanks for additional interviews and technical, financial, and moral support also go to the ADCO Foundation, Samantha and Maryanne Armer-Yenouskas, C. J. Baehr, Robert Baehr, Teana Baehr, Phoebe Bender, Bea Blair, Jacquie Bishop, Daphne Busby and the Sisterhood of Black Single Mothers, Chris Choy and Third World Newsreel, Becky Chalker, Jim Clapp, Marcia Corbett, Ginger Elvin, Michelle Gechlick, Faye Ginsburg, Ethel Gobles, Gayle Gorman, Jim Hough, Laura Kaplan, Flo Kennedy, Norma Lazore, Beatrice McClintock, Barbara McGaughlin, Joan Nestle and the Lesbian Herstory Archives, Melissa Nwaka, Adrienne and Martha at Paper Tiger Television, Katy Rich, the Paul Robeson Fund, Lynn Paltrow, Roz Petchesky, Ron Piniero, Julie Reeder and the CLEC Canvass Network, Helen Rodriguez-Trias, the Sophia Fund, the SUNY-Binghamton Pro-Choice Coalition, Ann Snitow, Sarah Tietze, the Unitarian Universalist Social Concerns Grants Panel, Dell Williams, Brady Wiseman, and Debbie Zimmerman and Women Make Movies.

INTRODUCTION

For the past two years I have been running "Abortion Rap" workshops with young women in the reproductive freedom movement. *Abortion Without Apology* grows out of this work. It uses history to encourage a new generation of activists to envision what they really want, and to empower them to take action to get it.

The stories of the women in this pamphlet are in danger of being lost to history. If their stories are hidden, contemporary activists will be left without an understanding of how we arrived at this critical moment in history, and will be forced to reinvent the wheel. Knowledge of the history of abortion policies and politics is critical to today's reproductive freedom movement.

Until the early 1880s, when most states passed severe anti-abortion laws for the first time, abortion was not illegal in this country. The evolution of anti-abortion policy was shaped primarily by the developing medical profession. With the establishment in 1847 of the American Medical Association (AMA), doctors gained an organizational and lobbying vehicle through which to mount effective legislative pressure. They succeeded eventually in outlawing most abortions, a situation that remained unchanged and virtually unchallenged for nearly a century.

Their even more ambitious crusade to monopolize the female health care market is well documented in books on the history of women and medicine (see Bibliography). In the early decades of the 19th century, "regular" physicians (the elite who had been to even a few months of medical school) had begun to perceive female patients as the gateway to family practice—and they saw "irregular" physicians (homeopaths and others critical of the European-trained "regulars") and midwives as obstacles in their paths. Discrediting these practitioners, who had traditionally provided obstetrical and gynecological care—including abortion—was their ticket to the higher status (and incomes) delivered by professionalization.

At the same time, the developing white middle class elaborated a "cult of domesticity." This set of ideas about gender's place in social life specified that men and women inhabited separate spheres: women were in charge of the private sphere of household and family while men controlled the rest. For women, this division of labor encouraged quality rather than quantity motherhood, which in turn increased the demand for abortion as middle-class couples tried to limit the number of children they would have.

Doctors capitalized on eugenics arguments and provoked alarm about the destructive potential of female sexuality in order to incite public condemnation of conscious family limitation. Passage of the Comstock Law in 1873 gave a boost to the doctors. This law, passed without a word of discussion in Congress, banned obscene materials—including literature about birth control or contraceptive devices—from the mails. But it was only after concerted lobbying efforts by the AMA, state medical societies, and their allies among Catholic and Protestant clergy that state legislatures outlawed "criminal" abortions—abortions not clearly required to save a woman's life. In New York state, for example, the Medico Legal Society drafted a bill in 1872 which defined providing or obtaining an abortion as a felony. It was adopted almost verbatim by the state legislature. But until the doctors' campaign geared up during the 1860s and 1870s, the practice of abortion before "quickening" (approximately the end of the first trimester) was widely condoned. In fact, it was understood in just about the same way we understand miscarriage today. Since pregnancy itself was not confirmable, the elimination of an unquickened fetus was considered a matter of very little significance.

The AMA campaign against abortion, which aimed to change such casual public attitudes as well as alter the law, was based on the assumption that if doctors exerted authority over abortion decisions and practice, they would exert more authority in general. The campaign succeeded because doctors managed to convince male politicians—and the middle-class male public—that abortion was a serious threat to the maintenance of patriarchal authority. Controlling women's reproductive choices through the innovative tactics of state regulation and criminalization of abortion was, the doctors claimed, a necessary precondition of social order itself.

Despite the new laws, women continued to terminate unwanted pregnancies. As social and economic conditions compelled both middle-class and working-class women to limit their fertility, the birth rate fell from an average of 7 births per woman in 1800 to 3.5 in 1900. Although not all of this dramatic decrease was accounted for by abortion, the well-publicized arrests of prominent abortionists and the booming abortifacient business of the 1840s suggests that women sought abortions in rising numbers during the first half of the 19th century. As late as 1870, women could procure abortions in Boston or New York City for as little as $10. But the spread of criminalization in the 1880s took

Introduction

reproductive control away from women and gave it to doctors, and things stayed that way for almost a century.

In 1959, the American Law Institute (ALI), a national non-profit organization whose goal it was to "rationalize" legal process, drafted a model statute that expanded the conditions under which a woman might be granted an abortion. The ALI bill would permit abortion in cases where the woman could convince a hospital "therapeutic abortion committee" that her pregnancy had resulted from rape or incest, that it endangered her life or her physical or mental health, or that the fetus was deformed. The ALI bill was first introduced into a state legislature in California in 1961. Although the bill did not pass until 1967, it enjoyed increasing support among professionals in the early 1960s. During those years, a thalidomide scare and a rubella epidemic drew public attention to the demand for abortion on grounds other than preserving the life of the mother. This bill did not speak to the needs of the majority of women seeking abortions, however, and as a result it did not generate much grassroots support.

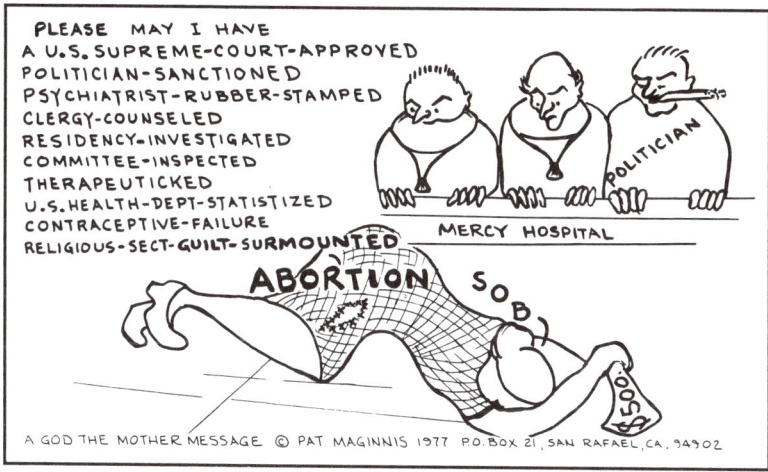

The radical history presented in this pamphlet begins in 1959 with the story of the Army of Three, the first U.S. activists to advocate the complete *repeal* of abortion laws and restrictions. The Army of Three—Patricia Maginnis, Lana Clarke Phelan, and Rowena Gurner—organized before the "second wave" of feminism exploded in the late 1960s. They were the first activists to talk about abortion in terms of *women's* rights. By addressing themselves to ordinary women rather than to doctors and legislators, the Army of Three began to build a grassroots movement that asserted that women—not legal and medical professionals—should make decisions about abortion.

The abortion law repeal work begun by Pat, Lana, and Rowena was carried on most successfully in New York in 1970. The New York fight took place under a historically specific set of circumstances: a falling birth rate; later marriage and childbearing among young women; rising college and labor force participation among women; a rising divorce rate; an increase in female-headed households; continued low wages for women; and civil rights and anti-war movements that demonstrated how ordinary citizens could take power over their own lives. These conditions provided an increased need for abortion and helped catalyze women to fight for their own liberation, including control over their own reproduction. The women's liberation movement mushroomed in the late 1960s and early 1970s, and the abortion issue both drew women into feminism and emerged as a focus of feminist activism. Feminists analyzed abortion policy in terms of men's power over women. They called their position "pro-abortion."

The work of pro-abortion activists helped win abortion law reforms in New York in 1970 and nationally in 1973. These reforms were a compromise of the demand for repeal: the complete elimination of abortion laws. The Supreme Court's *Roe v. Wade* decision that legalized early abortion in 1973 expanded the conditions under which a woman might be allowed an abortion, but it stopped short of endorsing the idea that each woman had the absolute right to control her own body no matter what. Rather than leaving the abortion decision up to each woman, the Court stated that the decision to abort was protected by the right to privacy between a woman *and her doctor* and it stated that the government could restrict or even prohibit abortion under certain circumstances. It gave women an abortion policy which was controlled by the state and by doctors, not by women seeking abortions.

In *Roe v. Wade,* the Court did not decide that women had the *right* to abortions, especially if they could not pay for them. After *Roe,* however, most middle- and working-class women could buy abortions. Since they could get their own needs met, most did not continue to work on abortion or related reproductive issues. Poor women and women of color were left to organize on their own behalf around issues that affected them (such as sterilization abuse) but that did not generally affect and therefore did not activate the bulk of the women who had made up the women's liberation and pro-abortion movements.

In the mid-1970s, legal restrictions began to chip away at women's access to abortion. Not surprisingly, the first restrictions (such as Medicaid abortions, prisoner's abortions, young women's abortions) did not affect the majority of middle-class white women, and (again not surprisingly) middle-class whites did not mobilize to fight these restrictions in

Introduction

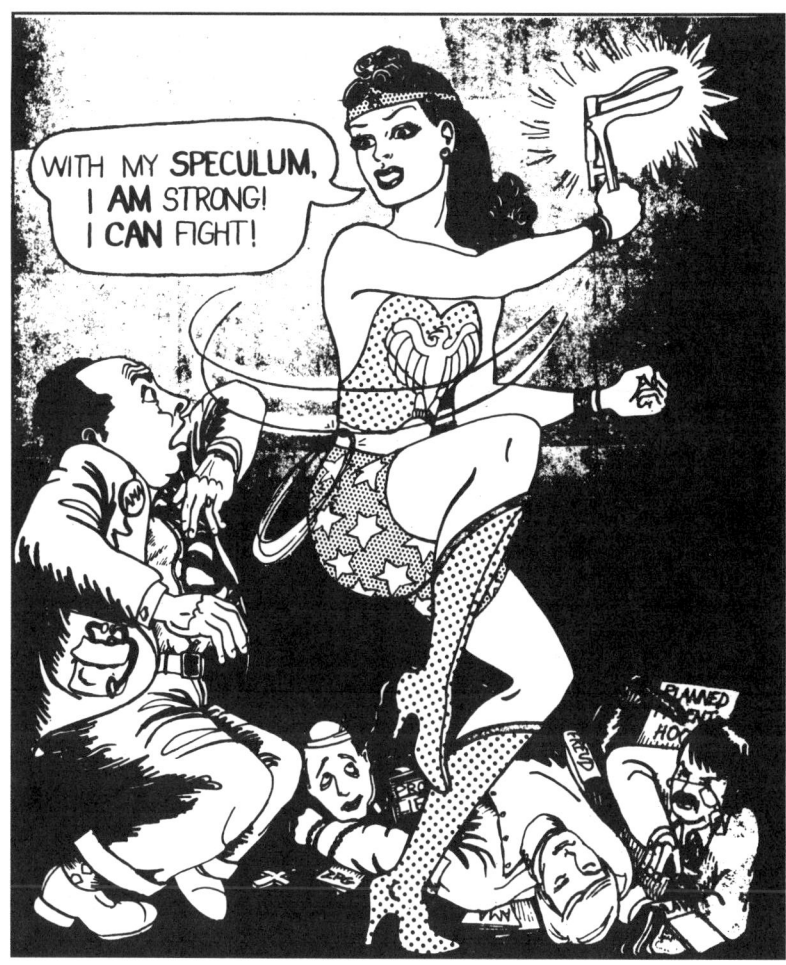

large numbers. Those who had the foresight to spot the trend that would eventually jeopardize their own interests generally responded not by joining a broad reproductive rights movement, but rather by focusing on the single issue that could most directly affect them: "legal" abortion. Abortion organizations in the late 1970s and 1980s very often did not link abortion to other reproductive rights or to women's liberation. With the women's movement dwindling and the political climate shifting to the right, many such groups turned to single-issue organizing in an attempt to defend the gains that had already been made. In an effort to soft-sell abortion in changing political times, activists adopted the term "pro-choice," a move some veteran organizers claimed made abortion "the right that dare not speak its name."

The erosion of abortion rights that began in the 1970s reached critical proportions in the late 1980s. The 1989 *Webster* decision threatened to restrict access to abortion even among middle-class women and finally galvanized that population to take action. Some women joined pro-choice groups that continued to concern themselves only with abortion. Others became involved with women's groups that addressed abortion in terms of men's power over women. Still others looked beyond this analysis to a goal of reproductive freedom.

A reproductive freedom agenda requires that women have the right to express themselves sexually; live free from the threat of sexual harassment or violence; become parents; abstain from parenting; use safe, effective contraception; obtain abortions; be free from forced sterilization; enjoy quality medical care; have access to good childcare; work and live in safe environments; and receive quality sex education. It demands these things for all women; therefore it requires that each woman be free from oppression, including oppression based on sex, race, class, sexual orientation, or physical ability. The reproductive freedom agenda is a radical agenda.

In this pamphlet, I generally apply the term "liberal" to the ALI/reform and pro-choice movements, and the term "radical" to the repeal, pro-abortion, and reproductive freedom movements. "Radical" means "at the root." Historically, "radical feminism" has described the belief that sex is the first oppression from which all forms of oppression stem, that by working on sexism one works on all "isms." Here, I use "radical" to imply a demand for a revolution in the balance of power. I describe as radical those activists whose ideas and actions demand that women— not doctors and lawyers—have ultimate authority over their own bodies and their own lives. Their example proves that women have every right to make life-and-death decisions. And it inspires us to continue working for a vision of total liberation.

This pamphlet is based on 25 audiotaped, videotaped, and filmed interviews with pioneers in the fight for reproductive freedom. It is designed as an organizing tool. The first three chapters describe the radical history of the abortion movement. The fourth chapter summarizes the general lessons of the past. The fifth chapter suggests organizing strategies for the future. This pamphlet also contains a selected bibliography and a brief list of reproductive freedom resources. *Abortion Without Apology* may be used alone or as a companion to the film documentary "With A Vengeance" by Lori Hiris. "With A Vengeance" is available from Women Make Movies, 225 Lafayette Street, New York, New York, 10012, (212) 925-0606.

1

The Army of Three

Making Abortion Public

The radical U.S. movement for abortion began in 1959 when a woman in California named Patricia Maginnis got pregnant for the third time. Pat Maginnis was a very fertile woman, but she did not want to have children. The first time her contraception failed, she went to Mexico, where abortions were illegal but relatively available. When she came back, she swore she would never again leave this country for medical care she considered to be her right.

One year later, Pat's contraception failed again. Pat didn't know how to find a safe illegal abortionist in the United States, but she did know enough about her own body to figure out how to try to end her pregnancy herself. She stuck a catheter—a hollow piece of plastic tubing—up her vagina, through her cervical os, and into her uterus. She gave herself a terrible infection and nearly died in the process, but in her sixth month she did finally miscarry.

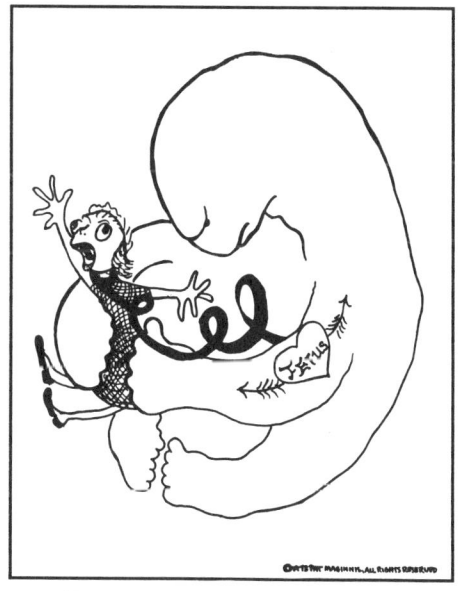

The very next year, Pat's contraception failed again. She still didn't know how to find a good illegal abortionist, but she did have a better idea of how to end her pregnancy herself. She didn't want to run the risk of poking a catheter into her uterine walls again, so this time she put a finger through her cervical os, the neck of the womb. In the years to come, a more sterile version of this "digital method" of do-it-yourself abortion was one of Pat's most controversial organizing tools.

By the time she had terminated her third pregnancy, Pat was outraged at what needing an abortion meant for women. In a letter solicited for this pamphlet, she described her experience at San Francisco General Hospital when she admitted herself for post-abortion care:

> I was put in a ward devoted entirely to botched abortion cases. A few days into my stay in that ward, two plainclothes inspectors interrogated me about the details of how I got my abortion. They told me... that I had no civil rights, no right to silence... I was further instructed to contact them when I got out of the hospital. Two weeks later, at home, I received a phone call from one of them asking why I had not followed their instructions and contacted them. I replied that an attorney had instructed me that it was not necessary for me to contact them. The homicide inspector asked, "Who told you that?" To which I replied, "Ernest Besig from the American Civil Liberties Union." Whereupon the homicide inspector slammed down the phone.

Pat wanted to change abortion laws but, she wrote, "At that time even mentioning the word abortion was taboo and the mass media avoided the word completely. In California it was a felony even for the medical profession to discuss abortion techniques." Pat's first step was simply to start people talking about abortion. In the early 1960s she began a one-woman campaign. Standing alone on street corners, she conducted the first public opinion poll on abortion ever organized in the United States. By speaking to people individually and later in groups, Pat began to lay the foundation of a grassroots abortion rights movement.

For all her originality, Patricia Maginnis might never have become the West Coast catalyst for the abortion movement had it not been for the organizational talent of Rowena Gurner. While Pat insists that it is not necessary for a woman to experience an abortion to support reproductive freedom, Rowena describes her interest in the abortion movement as purely personal. As a young woman, she got pregnant through contraceptive failure and had a successful but painful, frightening, and expensive abortion in Puerto Rico. In the early 1960s DC-9s to Puerto Rico were so frequently filled with women flying south for dilation and curettage abortions that the trip was sometimes referred to as the "D&C Express." In an interview Rowena vowed, "Whoever made me go through this, I was going to make them pay!" She explained:

I flew to Puerto Rico. The abortion itself was not bad. The circumstances surrounding it were horrendous. I had developed a terrible case of the flu and was running a high temperature on the plane. I thought to myself, "If this person really is a doctor and sees how terribly ill I am, perhaps he won't want to do the abortion!" In addition, I had to be back at my job exactly on time as my boss had threatened to fire me if I took any extra time for my "vacation."

The abortion cost more than twice what I had been told. I wanted to return home immediately to save money, but the doctor (who was truly a doctor) advised me to stay in Puerto Rico until the last minute. In that way, if I encountered unexpected problems, he could treat me. This was the very first kind, humane thing that was said to me.

Well, I was absolutely infuriated by the entire experience. I could hardly believe it! No one was really interested in me or this embryo or fetus or whatever, but everyone and every law conspired to make this abortion as much of a problem and as terrifying as possible. "Someone would pay for this," I vowed. No one could put me through this agony and get away with it! I thought about it and thought about it... for years! I couldn't stop thinking about it! I rode my bike from New York to California the following year, thinking about it the entire time. I settled in Palo Alto where I joined the Ethical Culture Fellowship. It was composed of very liberal, educated people, and I hoped that through this group I could do something (I didn't know what!) about abortion.

A woman in that organization had met or heard of Pat Maginnis. Knowing of my interest in abortion, she obtained Pat's telephone number for me. Now, basically, I am not a joiner, preferring to do everything on my own. Each week, this woman asked me if I had gotten in touch with Pat. Each week, I said, "No." I never realized that a meeting might be profitable.

So that I could finally say "yes," I did call and arrange to meet with Pat. I went to the apartment where she lived and, in her spare time, worked on the abortion issue. It was at that meeting with Pat, or possibly the next one, that Pat showed me a letter she had received from someone in New York. The letter was all about abortion. I looked up at Pat when I finished and said, "Fine. Where's the answer?"

Pat: I haven't answered it yet.

Me: (Looking at the date of the letter) But it's dated...

Pat: Yes.

Me: (I am extremely compulsive.) Would you like me to answer it for you?

Pat: That would be nice.

I type out the answer, show it to Pat who reads it and approves. Pat holds out a second piece of paper, saying, "Here's another letter..."

In this way, Rowena became "the general" of the abortion movement. She said, "Before I knew it I was at Pat's place constantly, playing around with the abortion movement. But it wasn't playing, it was real." She was distressed to discover that Pat had been funding "the movement" out of her own shallow pocket and taking on almost all of the work alone. She determined to make the abortion movement self-supporting and efficient. Unlike the better established pro-choice organizations of today, Pat's group was run not by administrators but by activists. As a result, it operated on a shoestring budget. The core members continued to pour their own time and money into the movement, but after Rowena took charge the group did begin to generate some funds.

Initially, Pat had no interest in the band-aid work of providing abortion referrals. Her goal was to eliminate all laws restricting abortion. Most people were not yet prepared to speak out for this cause, however, and the women who came to Pat were mainly interested in ending unwanted pregnancies. When Rowena joined Pat in 1964, she immediately saw the value of using underground referrals as an organizing tool. Once she took charge, women seeking referrals were required to donate five dollars and two hours of office work to the movement and to write and sign pro-abortion letters to their legislators.

In addition to managing money, Rowena "managed" the image of the abortion movement to make it appear respectable. Given the taboo surrounding abortion, she believed that presenting an air of respectability would help the cause. She solicited the support of "pillars of the community" whenever possible and insisted that anyone representing the movement look conservative and sedate. She also did her best to "manage" Pat's image and her public appearances. Pat has always lived simply, giving away any extra money to political causes and friends in need. Her taste in dress is unconventional, and Rowena took over her "speaking shopping" as well as her scheduling. Pat is a powerful orator, and by 1965 she was speaking out for abortion throughout California. In her free time she continued to ask people's opinions about abortions and to hand out pro-abortion fliers on street corners.

In 1965, Pat spent an afternoon standing in the rain in San Francisco passing out leaflets to men and women who were leaving a conference on world hunger. One of the women, Lana Clarke Phelan, grabbed a flier as she ran to her car to drive 450 miles south to her home outside Los Angeles. When she got there, she uncrumpled the wet mimeographed sheet and saw the words REPEAL ABORTION LAWS in big letters at the top and a little blurb on abortion laws and on pro-abortion articles distributed by Pat and Rowena underneath. Lana had a keen interest in abortion laws that was born out of personal experience:

NEWS MAGAZINE TALKS ABOUT DO-IT-YOURSELF ABORTION WITH PATRICIA MAGINNIS

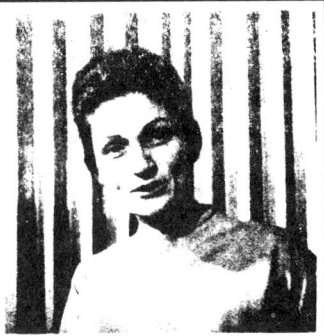

"Are you pregnant? Is yours a wanted pregnancy? If not, why not see an abortion specialist?" These jolting questions head a mimeographed instruction sheet distributed by Patricia Maginnis

"Abortion Clinic" recently staged in La Jolla by the San Francisco obstetrics technician.

Here Miss Maginnis discusses with NEWS

I was a Depression kid, born in 1920. And we were poor. Just very, very poor. I was married when I was fifteen years old. I lived in Florida. That was in the teeth of the Depression. People old enough to remember the Depression will remember how poor everyone was. I suppose that anyone who would feed a girl, it was that much less for the family.

I married a man ten years older than I was. He was a good man. Good enough. Nothing wrong with him, except that he should have known better than to marry a fifteen year old. I was so woefully ignorant about sex! I didn't know what was happening to me. I certainly didn't enjoy it. All I knew was that in a month, I was pregnant. Ten months later I had a baby girl, a very, very hard delivery, some three days in labor, and doctors and nurses tipeetoing in and out saying, "Is she dead yet?" And I was thinking, "No, I'm not dead yet. I can still hear you." And I did, as you can see, recover.

I had a very tiny little jaundiced baby with her little head all misshapen from all those hours of labor. I was scared to death of that baby! I didn't know how to take care of her. I thought she wasn't going to breathe. I'd go in at night to make sure she was still breathing.

Anyway, when I left the hospital, the doctor said, "Don't ever get pregnant again, because you won't live through it." But he didn't tell me how *not* to get pregnant. And, human nature being what it is, three months later I was pregnant again.

I was scared to death! I had this little tiny, tiny baby, and nobody to take care of her except me. And here I was. I was going to die! Well, I thought this over. I didn't want to die. And I didn't want to leave that child alone. I did what women are having to do and have had to do for centuries. I knew there had to be some way to stop a pregnancy. Had to be. But nobody would talk about it. It wasn't something you could discuss.

I was working at the Walgreen drugstore in the tea room, and I asked the other women who worked with me, all of whom were older than I was and they told me about abortion. But they didn't know where it could be done. I finally landed in a conversation with the cosmetologist in the store and she told me about a midwife, a Cuban midwife in Ybor City, which is a suburb of Tampa and was at that time a Cuban settlement. And I went out to see her. She told me she would do it for $50.00.

Well that was a real blow, because at that time I was working for $7.00 a week, and that was supporting a whole family. There was no way in the world for me to get that much money. But I had to get that much money.

I did not tell my husband. He was not a man who could handle things. I didn't tell anybody. This was my secret. It was my responsibility. And if I had to account to God for it, then so be it. I'm just telling you how my mind worked at that time. This is a woman's problem, and that is why women have to have the last word, the absolute last word, on these things.

Anyway, I sold things. I sold my dishes that I had gotten, nice pieces to start a set. I sold a little ring I had. I saved my money. I went without food, I remember that! And I finally got $35.00.

By that time I must have been about three months pregnant. Maybe a little more. I went back to the doctor, and he said to me, "I told you not to get pregnant. Well, now that you are, I'll see if I can keep you alive." Very condescending. Not very cheerful. And that was when I really had to start looking for help in earnest.

I knew I needed the $50.00, and I had $35.00. I borrowed the other $15.00 from a very nice man who was a customer at the store. He ran an auto agency, and I figured he was rich. I asked him to lend me the money, and I told him I couldn't tell him why. He may have known why I needed it. I don't know. Anyway, he let me have it, and I had my $50.00.

By that time I had gone much, much too far. I really should have had help immediately. But I had my $50.00 and I went back out. And this woman, her name was Mrs. Urga. I can say it now because I'm sure she is long gone. Mrs. Urga packed my cervix with some kind of an insertion. Maybe slippery elm? I don't know what it was. She poked it up my cervix, and she told me to go home. In a couple of days I would have pains, my menstrual period would start up, and everything that was in me would drain out, and I would no longer be pregnant. And she told me not to come back there.

I went home, and I went back to work, and two days later I was doubled over with cramps and really in pain and running a temperature. I knew that something was happening to me, but still, no blood, no spotting. And so I went to some relatives' house for dinner that night. The whole family was there. And none of them, of course, knew what was going on with me. And I could not and would not tell them. But at the table I could no longer contain this pain, and I excused myself and went into the bathroom.

I had blood all over my underwear. I sat on the toilet and tried to clean the blood off myself with water. And then I saw a tiny little limb. I don't know if it was an arm or a leg but a little tiny protrusion coming out of my vagina. I was absolutely horrified. I was paralyzed with fear. And I couldn't tell anybody. And I certainly couldn't have this happen in my sister-in-law's bathroom!

I cleaned myself up as presentably as I could and went back and told the family that my head hurt, I had a sick headache, and would they excuse me, I needed to go home. They wanted to go with me but I told them to stay and finish their dinner. I got outside and found a taxi, and with all the money that I had I went back to Ybor City.

It was so dark. I went around the side of this woman's little shack. Through the bushes. Scared to death, but more afraid not to go than to go. I went to the side door where I had been before. I knocked hard and she came to the door and said, "I told you not to come back here again." And I said, "I had to." I was crying, and she let me in. She had a little surgery room that was relatively clean for those days; clean sinks, and a clean little gurney with fresh white paper on it. She put me up on the gurney and checked me and said, "Well, you're almost done." And she finished me up and took this little mass out of me.

After she had cleaned me up, she came around the gurney and put her arms around me. This great big woman, big Black woman, with these big, motherly arms, and, you know, a wonderful warmth about her. And she put her arms around me and she said, "Honey, did you think it was easy to be a woman?" Those words have stayed with me years and years. I can still hear them. I'll never forget that woman. She was so kind.

I left, and as I did, she said, "This time don't come back, because if you do, you'll get me in trouble." And so I went home. I had fever for a couple of days. And maybe because I was young and resilient, I got well. Afterwards, I went back to that doctor, that Ob/Gyn who had said he'd try to keep me alive, and I said to him, "I had an abortion." And he put me up on the table and he checked me out and he said, "Good job. I figured you were a smart girl and would get out of it one way or another." Well, I didn't have a vendetta when I first walked in to see him, but...!

As soon as Lana saw Pat's flier, she sent away for all the pro-abortion literature it advertised and began a regular correspondence with Pat and Rowena. Later that year, Pat called Lana and asked her to deliver a pro-abortion speech in Southern California. Pat didn't have enough money to pay for transportation, and Lana was the only abortion advocate she knew of in the Los Angeles area. Lana felt totally unprepared, having only her own experience and Pat's little pamphlets to draw on, but she agreed to speak and thus became the Southern California representative of the pro-abortion movement.

Lana is no one's picture of a radical. In 1965, she lived with her second husband, a police officer, and worked as a legal secretary. She lost her job as a direct result of speaking out about abortion. With her husband's full financial and moral support, she became the movement's first full-time activist.

Today, Pat, Lana, and Rowena are sometimes called the Three Crusaders or the Army of Three. The Army of Three knew that they had to do more than get people just to talk about abortion. They wanted to eliminate abortion laws. The only way they knew how to do this was to break a law, get arrested, and get sentenced. This would be challenged on the grounds that the law was unconstitutional.

In a letter solicited for this pamphlet, Rowena explained how they tried to get arrested:

> Pat and I produced (an illegal) list of "abortion specialists." Most of these specialists were located in Mexico. At first the list contained less than a handful of names. We gathered as much information on the specialists as possible. As the weeks went by, people who learned of our list sent in additional names and information. In this way, the specialist list was constantly updated and expanded. Included with this list was a sheet of questions. Any woman who obtained an abortion was urged to answer the questions on this sheet. The information requested was comprehensive. The woman who answered the questions and sent in the sheet was not asked her name or address. In this way, we were able to update the list with the very latest information. Thus the original one-sheet list eventually ran well over 20 single-spaced typed pages. It was designed to answer every possible question a woman might have about her abortion including tests for pregnancy and post-abortion care.
>
> The lengthy list was mimeographed. The first list had the words "Are You Pregnant?" at the top. This was changed depending on the situation. For instance, many of the lists were headed with a warning that the lists were updated on a daily basis, and that before attempting to use an abortion specialist the woman should send in for the very latest list. The list gave relevant information about the abortion specialist, for example, whether or not they spoke English, whether or not they were physicians, costs, hotels in the area and their charges, types of anesthesia, "before and after" abortion care, questions to direct to the abortion specialist if you were uncertain

of something. On two occasions, a patient seeking an abortion was raped by the doctor. This was noted on the list.

The Army of Three gave out thousands of referral lists. Apparently, however, the police hesitated to arrest the activists under laws that might, as a result, be declared unconstitutional. Or, Pat suggests, perhaps they just didn't want to get involved. She recalls:

> In about 1968 a Dr. McNulty, a Catholic and the chairperson of the California Board of Medical Examiners, was holding a hearing at the State Building in San Francisco to chastise nine prominent San Francisco doctors he accused of performing abortions. Rowena and I realized this was a fine opportunity to inform the public of available abortion services, underground and legal. At 9:00 am, at the start of the hearings, I gave out felonious (at that time) leaflets inviting the public to abortion classes. For 45 minutes, the police made no effort to enforce the law or to stop me from violating California Penal Code Section 267. A news reporter, frustrated by this delay by law enforcement officials, walked into the busy intersection where a blue-clothes cop was directing traffic. "That woman is breaking the law. Arrest her," said the reporter to the cop. "No," replied the officer, "I am directing traffic." The reporter approached me and said, "I am going to make a citizen's arrest..." After that, a police car appeared, and a cop drove me to the police station where I was booked but the officer refused to sign the arrest warrant! After an hour or so I was released on my own recognizance. The power elite was most reluctant to charge me with violating the [state abortion law and so] prosecuted me for breaking San Francisco Municipal Ordinance 188 [which prohibited distributing information on birth control, venereal disease, and abortion]. As a result of my case, this antiquated local ordinance was declared unconstitutional and dropped from the books.

A local ordinance was a small victory, but Rowena explained:

> Pat, Lana, and I wanted to be arrested for breaking state laws prohibiting abortions, aiding in obtaining abortions, and undergoing an abortion. Classes in abortion were conducted for this purpose. Each class lasted four hours. Classes were held weekends in cities and towns throughout California, in various large cities throughout the United States, and one night each week in my home in Palo Alto.
>
> Each abortion class was divided into four parts. In part one the abortion laws of the state were reviewed and explained. Attendees then had to write two letters to their legislators at the state capital demanding repeal of the abortion laws. During the second hour the women were advised on how to go to Mexico for an abortion there. All contraceptive techniques were also explained and contracep-

tive devices passed around. During the third hour the sterile technique was explained. The fourth hour was devoted to self-induced abortion. The "digital method" was thoroughly reviewed. By the time the class ended, the participants had an excellent understanding of the entire abortion problem.

Basically, these instructions [for the digital method] covered thorough cleaning of the bathroom and the woman herself, to maintain as sterile an area as possible. The woman was then to strip, put her hair in a hair net, clip the pubic hair, clip her nails, and then wash, wash, wash all areas with Lysol and/or Phisohex. Then, [by] squatting on the floor and pushing down as though to encourage a bowel movement, [she could] move the cervical os, the neck of the womb, close to the vaginal opening. The "digital method" involved the woman inserting one finger into the vagina and into the cervical os, the opening to the uterus. If the woman had previously given birth to a child, this area was soft and relaxed sufficiently to insert a finger. In many women, this area is completely unyielding, and the method is not possible. If the woman was able to insert a finger, the point was to try for two fingers, and then three. The opening to the uterus was to be made as large as possible and to be kept enlarged for as long as possible. A pregnancy cannot continue with the opening to the uterus kept enlarged. Eventually the woman would abort. The "digital method" could be done [once] daily, but preferably twice or more daily.

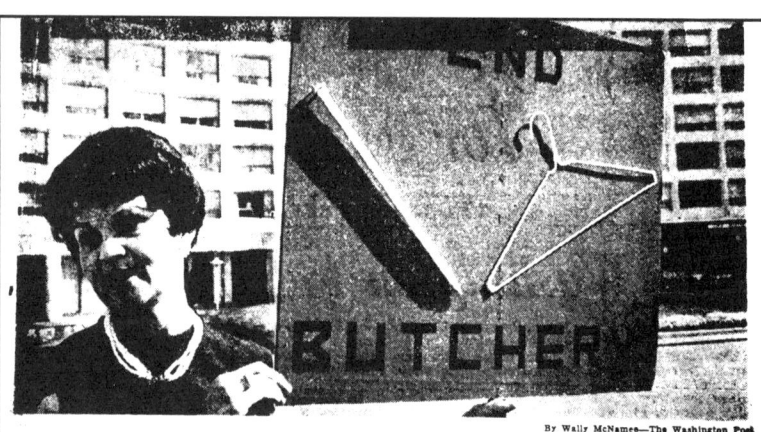

PICKETER—Lana Clarke Phelan of Long Beach, Calif., a member of the California-based Association to Repeal Abortion Laws, pickets the International Conference on Abortion at the Washington Hilton with a sign displaying a knitting needle and a coat hanger, items which she claims are commonly used in attempted self-abortions.

Abortion Class Draws Crowd

By Carol Honsa
Washington Post Staff Writer

Shyly, self consciously, reading of the District abortion law the anxious and the curious were overflowing tion for Repeal of Abortion Laws. DISPLAYING contraceptive products—and giving helpful hints on their be...

Once the woman started to abort, there was a problem of how soon she could go to the hospital to receive treatment. If she went too soon, the hospital personnel would joyously "patch up the pregnancy," a dreadful procedure if the woman wanted desperately to abort. The woman, therefore...had to be on her toes to evaluate what was going on and check her own temperature constantly to watch for infection.

Police were always invited to classes in the hope that an arrest would be made. Although police did attend, sometimes secretly in plain clothes, no arrests were made. Instead, the classes were welcomed and found to be interesting and informative. The classes continued for about a year, exhausting Pat, Lana, and me...

Finally, Pat read in the newspaper that the District Attorney of San Mateo County of California had declared that he would arrest us if we taught a class in his jurisdiction. Immediately, I scheduled a class there the following week. To be certain the police would not squirm out of making an arrest for "lack of evidence," I prepared "abortion kits" to be given out to attendees for that one class. Since the contents cost $2.00 per kit, the women attending classes were usually advised to assemble their own, but for this one class the ready-made kits would be "evidence." The kits were attractive and mysterious looking, containing (in a plastic see-through bag) Lysol, Phisohex, an orange stick, an emery board, nail clippers, a hair net, scissors, a thermometer, and instructions on the "digital method."

Pat and I arrived early at the apartment in San Mateo where the final—hopefully!—abortion class would be held. A huge drawing of women's internal organs was propped up. It had always been used in class. With luck, it could be another piece of "evidence." I suggested that the "digital method" be taught first to get the arrest underway. Pat agreed. The carton of "abortion kits" was placed in a prominent spot. The incriminating material was displayed in meticulous detail. The hour went by. Nothing happened. A man and a woman left the class. Pat and I groaned inwardly. What happened to the arrest? Would this never end? Pat asked the bewildered women to return the abortion kits that had been distributed. They were too expensive to give out without an arrest. [Finally] two people entered. The man and woman who had left had returned in police uniform... Pat and I were placed under arrest. We were so overjoyed, we almost sang on the way to the station house!

Although Pat and Rowena's case was not settled until after *Roe v. Wade* had effectively nullified such outmoded statutes, the Army of Three did finally succeed in having the California state law declared unconstitutional.

Pat's confrontational political strategies drew a great deal of public attention to her cause, and Lana's gift as an orator helped spread the word about abortion. Rowena's forte was organizing. In 1966 she put together the first pro-abortion conference ever held in the United States. Capitalizing on national attention focused on abortion when actress Sherry Finkbine and countless other women demanded abortions after taking thalidomide, she organized a distinguished panel on the subject. Four hundred and eighty-five people attended Rowena's conference, which was repeated in 1967, 1968, and 1969.

Throughout these years, Pat's original group, called the Society for Humane Abortion (SHA), continued to educate the public about the issue. To protect SHA's tax-exempt status as an educational organization, Pat and Rowena created the Association for the Repeal of Abortion Laws (ARAL) to carry on their political work. ARAL eventually grew into NARAL, the National Association for the Repeal of Abortion Laws.

Today, NARAL stands for National Abortion Rights Action League. In 1973, when the Supreme Court ruled on the *Roe v. Wade* case that liberalized abortion laws, NARAL had to decide whether to protect and defend the gains that had already been made, or whether to continue to press for the repeal—the complete elimination—of all abortion laws. NARAL's leadership opted to "keep abortion safe and legal" and changed the meaning of the acronym to reflect this shift in goals. Pat, however, had long been clear about the need to repeal abortion laws. In 1961, when the ALI (American Law Institute) bill was introduced into the California state legislature by Assemblyman John Knox, Pat tolerated the modest reform, but she recalls:

> The proposed Knox bill made me weep inside every time I read it. It was so awful, a sort of insult but a blessing, too... To read it was the bane of my existence. I got sick inside every time I had to look at it. But I had to look at it, because what else was there?[1]

By 1963, when the same bill was introduced by Senator Bieleson, she actively opposed the liberal reform. From that time on, Pat frequently proclaimed, "I am not out to legalize abortion! I am out to repeal abortion laws!"

By 1969, Pat had been a full-time abortion activist for nearly ten years. Still, abortion laws had not been repealed. In deep frustration, Pat and Lana wrote *The Abortion Handbook for Responsible Women*. Written tongue in cheek but, according to Lana, with tears in their eyes, *The Abortion Handbook* condensed information from the abortion classes into chapters with titles like "How to Reach Your Back Yard Abortionist," "Qualifying for Psychosis," and "Mrs. No-Money Goes to Hospital for

Clean-Up." The book provided practical information in a style designed to outrage:

- ### *FAKING THE HEMORRHAGE*

    From this moment on, we are pure fraud, and don't you forget it! We are going to make the best blood-and-guts hemorrhage we know how to put together, and present them with it at the county hospital. Unlike the woman who begs for an abortion on grounds of insanity, or rape/incest fun laws, and must face morality delays, the hemorrhaging woman and her physician know her condition will not wait for the legal moralists to carry on long discussions. Thus, if you appear on the hospital scene with a roaring hemorrhage, you stand a fair chance of getting abortion care without investigations, degradations, and rejections presently meted out by mediocre hospital abortion committees and smirking district attorneys.
    The first thing you need to know is where and how to borrow blood for your hemorrhage. So, as all women must, we turn to our kitchen for the ingredients.

    "Home-Made Hemorrhage Ingredients"

    2-3 lbs. of raw beef liver, freshly sliced

    1 small syringe (ear or infant)

    3-4 sanitary napkins

    Old clothing you can get very bloody

    1 taxicab...

    Wash your hands. Scrub your fingernails thoroughly. Examine beef liver. Don't wilt or collapse: blood is the stuff of life. Cut the liver into small pieces and squeeze every bit of blood into a clean bowl. Ideally, you need about three cups of blood. If there are clots, so much the better, so do not mash or destroy these. They give an authentic look to your efforts...Tuck a piece of plastic under your bottom so you won't ruin your rug or bedding. Lie flat on your back with your legs elevated. Prop up pillows if necessary. Tuck the mashed pieces of liver far up your vaginal tract. Take the little rubber syringe, fill it from your interesting bowl of hemorrhage-mix and squirt your vaginal tract full of as much blood as it will hold...
    If you have followed your instructions faithfully to this point, you will not really have to fake weakness and pallor. You already

look and feel sick! Acting a "life or death" role is always exciting, so expect an increased pulse rate and do not worry about your pounding heart. Appear worried, confused and very ignorant of everything. The medical profession loves the image of the dull, cow-like woman, so be what they want you to be.[2]

This technique, while no longer endorsed by Pat and Lana, is still used today by poor women seeking "emergency" D&Cs in states that do not fund medicaid abortions.

The Army of Three developed—without the benefit of a flourishing feminist movement—their confrontational, satirical style and their biting analysis of the position of a woman who needs an abortion. Their work preceded the second wave of feminism, but their analysis was always informed by their understanding of women's position in society and of the broader feminist issues involved in the abortion debate. Throughout *The Abortion Handbook*, Pat and Lana insisted that allowing men to make policy for women made as much sense as allowing dogs to make policy for cats. In a final chapter they concluded:

> Since your doggy-doctor is probably going to direct your reproductive role in a manner alien to your pussy-cat nature, you had better cease to be socially polite, deaf-mute and demand more respect. The womb is in your body, not his... you know what is best for you and yours. It's your body, your life, and your decision as to whether your pregnancy shall continue and you eventually bear an infant. Take charge of it now. Then and only then will you receive decent abortion care...[3]

Notes to Chapter 1

1. Schlesinger-Rockefeller Oral History Project Transcript of Interview with Patricia Maginnis, November 1975, p. 84.

2. Patricia Maginnis and Lana Clarke Phelan, *The Abortion Handbook for Responsible Women* (North Hollywood: Contact Books, 1969) pp. 119-121.

3. *Ibid.*, pp. 169-170.

Woman-Controlled Abortion

The Self-Help Health Movement

In 1969, Carol Downer, a Los Angeles mother of six, heard on the radio that a group of women had chained themselves to the White House to dramatize their demand for equal rights. Carol wasn't entirely certain what specific rights the women were demanding, but she was excited about the idea that it was possible for women to speak up for themselves, and she decided to attend the next meeting of the National Organization for Women (NOW). She said:

> There were quite a number of women there and they had an abortion task force. They had a little form and you indicated what your area of interest was. And since I had had an abortion and really knew how hard it was to locate someone and the whole ordeal, that's what I was most interested in. Lana Clarke Phelan was the chair of that task force, and I understudied her. I basically just trotted around after her and listened to her speak, and that was my training to learn about the history of abortion and to think about it.

California had passed an abortion reform bill in 1967, but legal abortions were still only available to women who could convince a hospital therapeutic abortion committee to give its permission. The Los Angeles chapter of NOW regularly provided referrals to an illegal clinic and some members had begun observing the procedure with an eye to opening an illegal clinic of their own. Carol said:

> The first woman that I observed was actually getting an IUD inserted, and for me it was quite mind-boggling because they put the speculum in and I looked and here was this extremely simple, beautiful structure, the cervix, and all of my agonizing and all of my

learning from Lana about the history—it just clicked! It was like, "Well, of course!" The only way that they can keep abortion illegal is to keep us in total ignorance of our bodies. Because once you see it you realize that abortion is so simple and so easy to do that any woman who has knitted and sewn and made pottery or done any of the multitude of things that women constantly do—we realized that we could do this. "This is nothing!" Mystifying us about our body was absolutely central to any patriarchal plan of keeping us down.

Los Angeles women who felt the way Carol did began a self-help health clinic at Everywoman's Bookstore. Carol said:

So that people would know what we were talking about—because remember we were still working on the idea of doing the abortions ourselves—we cleaned off a desk and I got up and did self-examination. And of course I hadn't the faintest idea what their reaction was going to be. I thought, "They are going to think I'm weird, I know! This woman is getting up and opening up her legs." I just had no idea how they were going to respond.

One woman at that meeting, Lorraine Rothman, recalled:

Carol said she had something really exciting to show us and that it had all kinds of ramifications as far as the direction of any work we would want to do. She said "Follow me" and took us into the next little adjoining room where there was a large desk, and she pushed everything off the desk and took her pants off and climbed up on the desk and showed us the speculum and immediately demonstrated how she could, herself, insert this plastic vaginal speculum into her own vagina, and with the use of a flashlight, a simple flashlight, and a hand mirror, she was able to see that portion of her body that had been inaccessible...
Carol showed us this plastic flexible straw-like device called the cannula, and said she had seen this used to do suction abortion in an illegal clinic in Los Angeles. The plastic straw-like device is simply attached to the end of a syringe with a tight fitting, and then, by pulling back on the syringe, suction is produced, and with this straw-like device through the cervix in the uterus, the contents of the uterus can be suctioned out. Well everyone was really excited about how simple this was. "Of course!"

Lorraine understood the power behind the idea of women doing their own abortions, but she could see potential problems with the instrument Carol demonstrated. The "Karman Cannula" developed by Harvey Karman, a psychologist turned abortionist, was primarily used by skilled illegal abortionists, including doctors. These "criminals" had frequent opportunity to operate the device. In the hands of unpracticed laywomen, it had several drawbacks. For one thing, it had to be held very firmly or it would jiggle and cause unnecessary cramping as suction was applied. For another, the syringe had to be detached from the tubing, emptied, and reattached to the tubing every time it got full. Lorraine was concerned that a woman might forget to return the syringe plunger to the correct position before reconnecting it to the tubing and accidentally force air into the pregnant woman's uterus. She said, "I went home and for the next week I started thinking about making it a little safer and

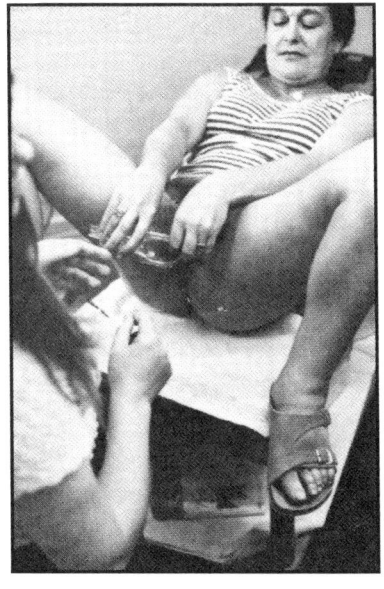

getting rid of some of these problems. And I started looking in the grocery store and the hardware store and the tropical fish store" A week later she came back with a mason jar, a cork with two holes in it, two lengths of fish tank tuning, and a syringe. These were the raw materials for the Del-Em, the suction device that became basic to what self-help proponents called "menstrual extraction." Menstrual extraction was the process by which a woman, with her self-help group, could remove the contents of her uterus—be it menstrual blood or early pregnancy.

In 1971, NOW invited Carol and Lorraine to attend a national NOW conference, where they demonstrated self-examination. Based on contacts they made at the conference, the two women mapped out a route and set out by bus on a tour of 23 cities around the country. When they pulled into a town, they would invite all the local women's groups to a meeting, demonstrate self-examination, and sell their little plastic speculums for two dollars. They also showed a home movie with a pregnant woman using menstrual extraction to show how simply an early abortion could be done by women who had acquired some basic knowledge about their reproductive anatomy. Invariably, they left a cluster of women planning a self-help group of their own. Some groups went on to learn how to do menstrual extractions. Like the Army of Three, however, self-help activists were not primarily interested in becoming abortion providers. They believed in the whole spectrum of reproductive freedom and did not see abortion as a single issue. Carol explained:

I think what we really need to have, first of all, is the recognition that a woman has the right to her own body. That means that she has the right to do self-examination if she wants, to have children if she wants, not to have children, to have sex if she wants, not to have sex, to be able to use condoms in her heterosexual relationships—to get the man to use a condom. If she has children, [she has the right] to expect this society to take responsibility to make sure that the child has good schools to go to, to support her in all the ways that anybody in this society deserves support for their children to grow up healthy and happy... I think that it is very broad. Our rights for this are not just to be able to go down to the abortion clinic and get an abortion. It's much deeper. This is absolutely not a single issue. It really goes right to the heart of our right to have our own sexuality. It's so fundamental. It is not just one issue among many.

You know, some people have said that it was a mistake, strategically, for women to focus in on abortion. But I think that if you understand that reproductive control is the issue, it becomes very logical that you must have the right to abortion and you must have access to maternity care and childcare and the whole string of things, but abortion is the first and foremost way we are having to work...

Once women started doing self-examinations, they immediately began to think of ways to solve problems. At that moment illegal

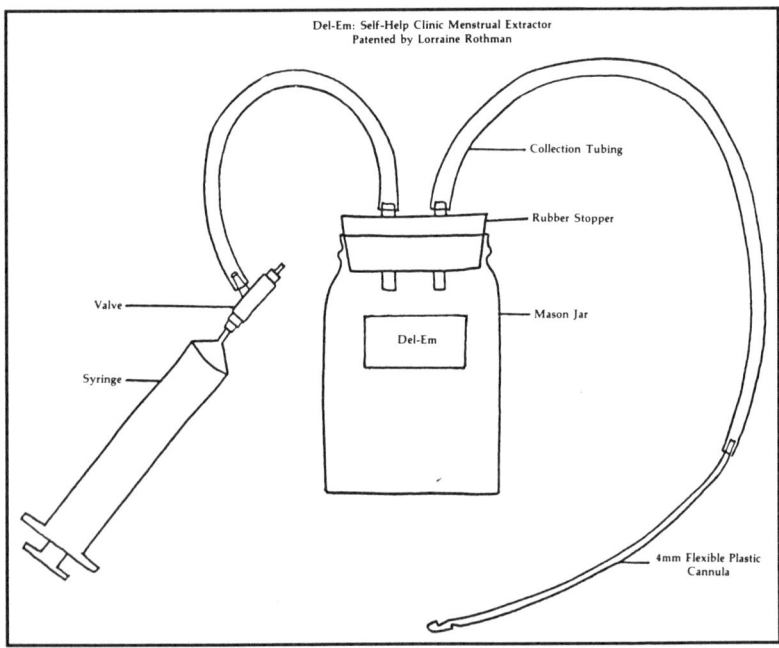

abortion was our main problem, so our main focus was going to be on how to overcome the fact that abortions were illegal in most of the country, so that's why abortion became our immediate thing.

Defining a problem and taking action to provide a solution is empowering. Some abortion rights activists defined anti-abortion laws as the problem and viewed legalizing or decriminalizing abortion as the solution. Others broadened their definition of the problem. Abortions were not only "criminal"; they were also dangerous, degrading, expensive, and hard to come by. While some activists petitioned legislatures and courts to solve the problem of illegality, others took direct action to solve the immediate problem of women with unwanted pregnancies. This was the case with JANE.

If you were a poor pregnant woman in Chicago in the early 1970s and you needed an abortion, you called JANE. JANE was a women's liberation abortion service that performed over 11,000 safe, affordable abortions between 1969 and 1973. JANE could help you when no one

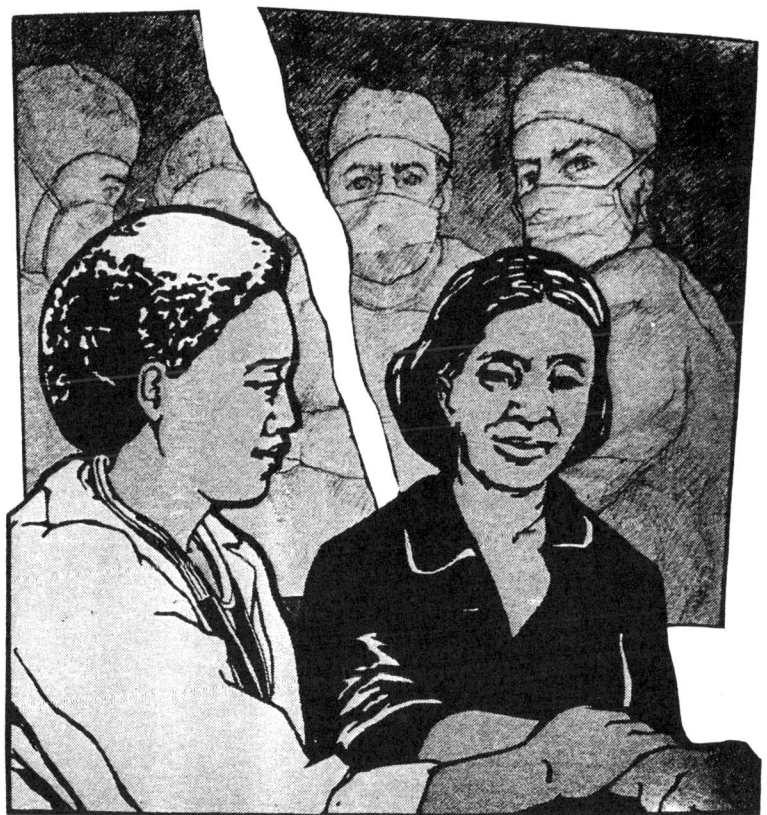

else would; at a time when most skilled abortionists charged between $300 and $2,000, this group asked for $100 and received an average of $40. JANE never turned a woman away for lack of funds.

You might get JANE's phone number from a free clinic, an underground newspaper, a sympathetic telephone operator, a friend, a doctor, even the cop on the beat. JANE was listed in the phone book under the last name "How." You called JANE, and JANE would tell you *how* to get an abortion.

JANE did D&C abortions and induced miscarriages. The service was started as a classic referral group by women who were neither doctors nor abortionists. They were mostly white middle-class housewives whose husbands supported them. Sometimes, the women who came to JANE for abortions came back to join the group. In later years, many of the women who joined JANE were young feminists who wanted to work in the women's liberation movement and who could live on very little money. (As one woman put it, "I was looking for this here women's movement that I'd heard so much about, and this was the booth I found to sign up at.")

Over time, the population JANE served changed. Women with money began to leave the state for their abortions once legal abortions became available in New York. Women without money stayed in Chicago. Most of the women who came through JANE were poor and Black. In an interview for this project, a former JANE member (who asked to be called "Jane") explained:

> The group spent a lot of time researching abortionists in the city of Chicago, and there were a handful of them. Most of them were no good. And they were no good because they were nasty, or they were not competent in terms of their technique. Mostly it was attitude...
> They did find this one abortionist who, as they all did, said he was a doctor. He was somebody who was competent in terms of his technique, very competent, but, you know, once you're dealing with illegal behavior, what you're dealing with is criminals, and these are, you know, sleazy people. Unpleasant characters. Not nice people, [but people] who are in it to make money. This guy was like that except that he was competent and very responsible. There was a number where you could reach him if you had problems, etc. And he was willing to work with this group.
> They started negotiating with him almost immediately on A) lowering the price and B) having more control. Instead of turning over a phone number to him, and [letting him] and his crew take it from there, [Jane] wanted to know more about what was going on with the woman. They didn't feel comfortable just sending women

off, basically. And he was willing to deal. And they made deals with him. You know, "We'll deliver so many women if you'll lower the price." Those kinds of deals. And there was a fortuitous set of circumstances so that it went from the women in the group not exactly knowing who did the abortions, to finding out that it was this person doing the abortions, to actually being around on the work days, setting up the work days. And doing pretty much all, everything except the procedure itself.

They slowly began to sit with women during the abortions. And then they slowly began doing some of the, what you might call medical, we called "technical" pieces, giving shots, inserting speculums, etc. Setting up, cleaning up, sterilizing equipment, that kind of stuff. So what happened was a slow, not very slow, but a slow process of evolution, and no major breaks except for a meeting at which it was formally disclosed, on pressure from group members, that in fact he wasn't a doctor. And at that meeting one of the members said, "Well, if he can do it, and he's not a doctor, then we can do it." And that time was really the crucial time. And that step which sounds so dramatic now really just made sense, because if we can do it, we charge a hell of a lot less.

What would happen is, we had this phone number: 643-3844, in fact. And a woman would call that number and get a tape and the tape would say, "This is Jane from women's liberation. If you need assistance leave your name and phone number and someone will call you back." And then someone would call her back, and the someone who called her back would say, "This is Jane. How can I help you?" And once that was established she would ask a series of questions about the woman's age, her last monthly period, a little bit about her pregnancy history, medical problems, tell her very briefly what the deal was. Those of us who did that call-back procedure, also had names of legal clinics in New York, or out of the country, or whatever, as other options. And then we would tell them that a counselor would get in touch with them fairly soon.

That information was then collected and put on three-by-five cards and passed out at our weekly meetings. The cards would pass around the room, and then they'd pass around again, and again, until most of the cards were gone. And then a particular counselor—if it was me, for instance, I would call the women whose cards I had and say "Hi," you know, use my name and say, "I'm gonna be your counselor. Let's figure out a time when you can come over, or I can meet you somewhere, and we can talk." And then the woman would normally come to her counselor's house, and we would sit around and we would drink a lot of tea and talk about the abortion. Make sure that she really wanted an abortion. Then we'd describe in detail what would happen to her on the day she would be scheduled, including where she would go, who she could bring with her, who would be there, step by step, as well as what would happen in the medical, the technical, procedure. And then we'd launch into our big birth control rap as well. We always described all the methods of birth control and talked a little bit about women and the health professions and how some of that worked. And anything that she wanted to talk about. Some women wanted to talk about the choice they had made and why they had made it.

Our aim was always to create a very loving, comforting supportive atmosphere, a reassuring atmosphere, to let this person know they were going to be alright. They weren't going to die. And they would probably be able to get pregnant the next year if they wanted to, or you know, soon, whenever they wanted to. And then that woman would be scheduled for a work day. We worked usually about three days a week. And she would be given the address of some place to go to. And this place we called "the front." Because it was a front [and not the place we actually performed the abortions]. It was always an apartment or house that belonged to one of us, or one of our friends, or somebody we knew who'd let us use their house for a day. The woman would be encouraged to bring anybody she wanted to bring. And she could bring her husband, she could bring her mother, she could bring her best friends, she could bring her kids, she could bring anybody she wanted to this place. We would schedule between twenty and thirty abortions a day.

So there would be these women, plus their "others," at this apartment or house. And there would be a lot of food. There would be, you know, tea and juice and cheese and crackers and cookies, and whatever. Oh, what I neglected to say is we would load her up with information as well. We had the old newsprint edition—I don't know if you've ever seen that—of *Our Bodies, Ourselves,* which I think we got for 25 cents a copy which we would give her, as well as a copy of *The Birth Control Handbook* and *The VD Handbook.* So we would load her up with stuff, and if she wanted extras for her friends, you know, our aim was really to get the information out. For many of us it was new information, and had really opened up our minds. And we wanted to get that information out and share it with as many women as possible. So, she would go to the front, and at some point during the day she would go in the car with just women who were going to have abortions—and usually about five women in a car load, mainly because we all had these little cars and we couldn't get more than five women and a driver in a car—and be taken to another place which was again an apartment or house that belonged to one of us or one of our friends or some person who was willing to let us use their place. And that's where the abortions would be done.

To "Jane," what is important about her story is not only that a group of women got together and did something, or even that they did solve an immediate problem for over 11,000 women. What is most significant to her is *the way* that the JANE group did what it did. A JANE pamphlet quoted in an unpublished article by Pauline Bart stated: "We are women whose ultimate goal is the liberation of women in society. One important way we are working toward that goal is by helping any woman who wants an abortion to get one as safely and cheaply as possible under existing conditions."[1] "Jane" said:

> We wanted to create an atmosphere that was empowering in a situation that was normally very disempowering...We wanted to give women some ammunition in their lives, and, by acting directly, show them that it was possible to take action in their own behalf and in behalf of other women. And do it successfully. And, I might add, at a great cost emotionally to everyone who was involved. It's very difficult working in a situation where you have no institutional sanction for what you are doing. And what you are doing is potentially life-threatening. So that you are always on that edge of whether you have a right to be doing what you are doing, but the need is just so great... There is always a place for people making decisions and acting on their own behalf and not turning over their own power to other people, whether because they have degrees or they have institutions or they have "the right." I think we feel too often in this world that we don't have the right to act in our own behalf. The most exciting thing for me always is to get together with a group of people and create something that addresses a need that's out there. That we do ourselves. And I think that's one of the greatest lessons of JANE. If there's something that needs to be done, we don't have to wait until x, y, and z happen. We don't have to beg anybody else to please do this for us. We can go ahead and we can do it ourselves.

"Jane" went on to explain:

> In the late 1960s, before abortion was even legal in New York, the issue of reproductive rights was tied into the awakening concept of feminism, the understanding that the right to control whether you're pregnant or not is indivisible from the right to self-determination about what you're going to do for a living, that the right to be a human being in the world is dependent on that right to be able to control your own reproduction. What I see now in the reproductive rights movement is that people really have sold out those values. I've seen other groups of feminists say, "We're not going to come out pro-abortion because we are going to alienate a lot of people..."
>
> I think the times were extraordinary. And it gave us the right to be more extraordinary in our action and activism... The timing was right. The times called extraordinary strength out of all of us and

changed us all. But we weren't by any means superwomen. We were lucky because we got a chance to put our politics into practice. The late 1960s and early 1970s was a river of action.[2]

JANE was raided by the police in 1972. Seven members were arrested. The charges were eventually dropped, but the crisis resulted in a shortage of skilled abortionists and made it even harder for JANE to meet the needs of women seeking abortions.

The idea of women controlling their own bodies, of taking power simply by acting as if they already had power, was tremendously threatening to the state and the medical establishment. Carol Downer was arrested three times. The most notorious case came to be known as The Great Yogurt Conspiracy. Carol was charged with practicing medicine without a license because she used the home remedy of applying yogurt to the vagina of a woman who was suffering from a yeast infection. The yogurt the police confiscated as evidence was someone's lunch. The lawyers argued about why it was okay to put a spoonful of chicken soup in a friend's mouth if she had a cold, but it was not okay to put a spoonful of yogurt in a friend's vagina if she had a yeast infection. Carol was acquitted, but the case illustrated the state's and the medical establishment's opposition to women learning to help themselves and to control their own bodies. Clearly, the government and the AMA favored state/doctor-controlled—not woman-controlled—abortion.

Regardless of what the government and the AMA have prescribed, women always have and always will break anti-abortion laws—some by having abortions, others by providing them. Some women break the law to prove a point. They commit civil disobedience with the full intention of being arrested and drawing attention to their cause. Other women break the law to provide needed services. They have no intention of getting arrested, either because they don't want to pay fines or go to jail, or because they have to remain free in order to provide the services that women truly need. Abortion activists have a rich history of taking the law—and their lives—into their own hands. When the law doesn't respect women, women won't respect the law.

Notes to Chapter 2

1. From an unpublished article by Pauline Bart, "Seizing the Means of Reproduction: A Feminist Illegal Abortion Collective—How and Why It Worked."

2. "Jane" quoted in "An Ordinary Group of Women," by Diane Elze, *Our Paper,* Winter 1987, pp. 12-13.

Speak Truth to Power

The New York Fight

If JANE was not a story about the bad old days of illegal abortion, my own abortion experience was not a story about the good new days of legal abortion. In 1980, when I was a 20-year-old in Montana, I had an abortion that made me very angry.

I went to a doctor a total of 17 times in one year so that my boyfriend and I could have sex without having children. My boyfriend went a total of zero times. (It hardly seemed fair that *I* was the one who got pregnant!) My boyfriend wouldn't wear a condom to back up my diaphragm. After a three-month, no-sex stand-off, he finally confessed that, at the age of thirty, he had never used a condom and didn't know how to put one on. Besides, he said, my insistence that he share the responsibility for birth control was really just a masked attempt to castrate him symbolically. I finally got on and then off the Pill, got one IUD (which came out), another IUD (which came out), and a third IUD, which left me pregnant.

My boyfriend had one "illegitimate" child he would not support or even see—but he still resented my making the abortion decision without consulting him. He believed that, as a relatively liberal man (for Montana), he had a right to participate in my decision. He even told friends that "we" were pregnant and that "we" were having an abortion. During the procedure, I kept wondering why, if "we" were having an abortion, I was up on the table (as usual) with my legs in the air, and he was out in the waiting room (for the first time!) with his legs safely crossed! Dealing with birth control and boyfriends made me pretty angry.

Dealing with my doctor also made me angry. I lived in a small town. There was only one doctor within 200 miles who would do abortions. He was very busy, and so he had a colleague put in the laminaria—the little stick of absorbent material that goes into the cervix the day before the procedure. The colleague told me I was killing a very real human life. I told him I really needed the abortion, so he let me get up on the table. Then he started sort of jabbing away at my insides. I began to cry. This must have been what he was waiting for. He dropped what he was doing, came out from between my legs, took my hand, and said, "Did you make the wrong decision, honey? Do you want to keep your baby?" I told him I was crying because he was hurting me, and I wanted him to finish what he was doing. Apparently he did not like my answer, because he went back down between my legs and smacked me a few good ones before he finally finished fitting the laminaria into the os. I cried all the way home.

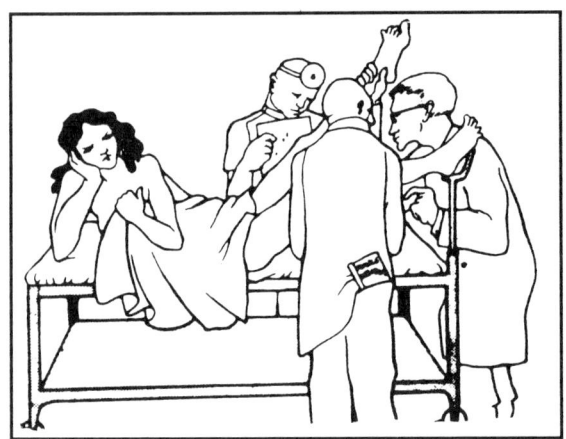

The procedure the next day was a relief. It was a little frightening, painful, and expensive, but it was definitely the right choice. Almost immediately, I began doing peer counseling with other young women needing abortions. After I got out of school, I began doing abortion rights work professionally.

By this time it was the mid-1980s. Feminism was out, Reagan was in, and abortion rights were very definitely under attack. A lot of us in the pro-choice movement believed that we needed to tone down our message, to "soft-sell" abortion to make it acceptable to the general public. In fact, the day I was interviewed by my state's affiliate of the National Abortion Rights Action League, I was told that it was fine that I was a feminist and, by now, a lesbian—but I shouldn't wear my politics on my sleeve. NARAL was a single-issue organization; I would be working with a lot of conservative (and, not coincidentally, well-heeled) supporters who didn't believe in a broader agenda for women's liberation.

On the job I discussed abortion not as a women's issue but as a civil liberties issue. I never talked about the related issues of reproductive and sexual control. I focused on the "hard cases" of rape, incest, and fetal deformity (remember the ALI bill?). I believed that, for women who chose it, abortion was a blessing—but I described it as a necessary evil. And I always assured everyone that abortion was a difficult decision for women—even though my own abortion had been extremely unpleasant but not morally problematic. I described pre-*Roe* abortions as horrible and legal abortions as wonderful—unless complications could be blamed on right-to-lifers. In short, I did not tell the truth about my own beliefs or my own experience.

Today, I am not paid to represent a particular point of view about abortion. Consequently, I get to say whatever I want. What I want is *free* abortions for all women who choose them. I want abortions to be available from lay practitioners as well as from doctors. I want an abortion to be accessible to every woman who wants one, no matter how small her town is, how young she is, or how many months pregnant she is. I want positive, supportive policies in federal, state, and local budgets and in Department of Health rules and regulations. I want the repeal of all abortion laws. And this, of course, is only the beginning.

These days, many of us wear buttons that say "Keep Abortion Safe and Legal." Because our radical history has been hidden from us, most of us who are under 35 do not realize that the legality we seek to defend was in fact a compromise of the original demand for repeal. If you repeal something from the law, you take it out of the law entirely. If you legalize something, you grant control to the state. For example, alcohol is legal in this country, but the government doesn't trust each person to regulate her own relationship with alcohol. It tells her how old she must be to drink it, when and where she may buy it—and it changes the laws about alcohol as it sees fit. This is not true of, say, orange juice. The criminal code does not mention orange juice. The government lets us drink it when, where, and how we want to. The FDA still checks to make sure that the orange juice is safe. The government will even help us pay for our orange juice if we receive food stamps. Other than playing this supportive role, the government is silent on the matter of orange juice. Repeal activists wanted the orange juice situation, not the liquor situation, when it came to abortion. They knew that as long as the government maintained a voice in each woman's abortion decision, it would use that power to chip away at women's right to abortion. Clearly, their predictions have come true with a vengeance.

The fight for repeal was a huge issue all across the country and, most especially, in New York state. In her peerless article, "The Power of History," Redstockings of Women's Liberation co-founder, Kathie Sarachild, wrote:

> It was in New York State, the area in which radical feminist analysis, action, and organization were strongest and most advanced, that the first concrete breakthrough of the women's liberation movement in the U.S. was achieved—the abortion law reform which for a few years turned New York State into "the abortion mill of the nation" and upon which the U.S. modeled its guidelines a few years later. It was the radical strategies of 1) opposition to reform and demand for repeal, led by Lucinda Cisler, 2) mass consciousness-raising on abortion with women testifying to their "criminal" acts in public and in court, 3) the development of the feminist self-help clinic ideas and their promotion of simpler, new abortion techniques that led to the national reform in five years time.[1]

This radical history has not been made available to the younger generation of pro-choice activists. As early as 1975, when Sarachild published "The Power of History" in *Feminist Revolution,* she noted:

> It has been only six years since the women's liberation movement mushroomed, and already the radical women who initiated the movement's theory, organizing ideas, and slogans, have been buried from public consciousness and the liberals have taken over, claiming credit for the radicals' achievements. If this goes on much longer feminism will go under once again—and we will lose almost all of what we have gained in the last years—both the radical consciousness and many of the practical reforms. It won't be too long now until the liberals will be gone, too.[2]

A young woman trying to track the history of the abortion rights movement in New York is up against a challenge. For one thing, the radical roots of the current reproductive freedom movement and the historical connection between the pro-abortion movement and the women's liberation movement are ignored by most existing pro-choice groups. The idea of looking to history for motivation and guidance is something she will have to come up with on her own. If she does try to find out about the past from such organizations, she may mistakenly be told that New York repealed its abortion laws in 1970, or that the U.S. Supreme Court recognized each woman's right to control her own body in 1973. In effect, she may be told that the revolution was won and that women got what they wanted. If she wants to know more, she will probably be referred to one of the only two books about the historic abortion battle in New York—*Abortion Two: Making the Revolution* by Lawrence Lader.

Lader is a historian, author, and 20-year veteran of the abortion rights movement. He was a driving force behind the creation of NARAL and is currently head of his own organization, Abortion Rights Mobilization. His book *Abortion Two* is an invaluable resource to students of the abortion rights movement. It provides a detailed account of the legislative battle over abortion and helps familiarize the reader with names, dates, and events significant to the fight. Like all books, however, it was written from a particular point of view—in this case the point of view of a man who saw himself as the leader of the movement. Women were the street troops, reform was almost as good as repeal, and people who thought otherwise were rabble-rousing extremists. The New York law was "an impossible victory."

A young historian may find her own way to *Aborting America,* the other book written about the struggle for abortion in New York. Like *Abortion Two,* this book also has a bias—in this case, the author, Bernard Nathanson, is a man who vied for leadership in the pro-abortion movement and eventually switched sides and became a superstar in the anti-abortion movement. The book is filled with slanderous comments (as one very small example, he compares Betty Friedan with a stack of tires) but it corroborates Lader's portrayal of ordinary women as troops and pawns in a battle masterminded by men.[3] Nathanson wrote:

> ...I considered abortion to be a broad social issue that feminists should not arrogate to themselves. Most important, I figured that if the feminists appeared to take over, necessary abortion reform would be dismissed by moderates without a fair hearing. I was dead wrong, of course. Lader's marriage with the feminist movement was a brilliant tactic.[4]

I intend to offer a different perspective on the battle for abortion rights in New York. I believe that the story of the abortion movement cannot be told apart from the story of the women's liberation movement and that "the impossible victory" was the first nail in the coffin of the fight for repeal. One of the lessons of the New York battle was that one could not be for complete freedom for women and also be for partial freedom for women—that reform is the enemy of radical change.

To understand what happened in New York, it is useful to know the legislative facts. Briefly, an ALI bill was introduced every year beginning in 1965. In 1968, when Ti-Grace Atkinson still headed NOW-NY, the organization's most powerful and radical chapter, the NOW-NY ad hoc abortion committee chairperson Ruth Cusack called Constance Cook, a Republican Assembly member from Ithaca, and asked her to introduce a repeal bill. Cook told Cusack that repeal had a snowball's chance in hell in a state that wouldn't even pass reform, but she agreed. In 1969, she and Franze Leichter, a Democratic Assembly member from New York City, introduced a bill intended to repeal all abortion laws from the criminal code. Both also signed on to the ALI reform bill, which failed again. When the ALI bill was defeated, Cook and Leichter took the opportunity to issue a press release stating, in part:

> The debate on the reform bill showed that many members were troubled by the moral and logical ambivalence of reform. Repeal will leave it to the individual and her doctor... to decide whether to proceed with an abortion.[5]

In 1969, when most abortions were still accomplished by D&C, and when the push was to have abortions performed by physicians rather than by butchers, it seemed reasonable to expect that decriminalizing abortion would mean that a woman would seek an abortion from her doctor. When Cook reintroduced the bill in 1970, she specified that abortions would be done by physicians—an unnecessary restriction, since pure repeal would have placed abortion in the same category as tonsillectomy, childbirth, contraceptive counseling, and other health-related practices which are not mentioned in the criminal code but which are governed by the Department of Health Rules and Regulations. In committee, the bill acquired two additional restrictions—a 24-week time limit, unless the woman's life was in danger, and a requirement that the procedure be performed with a woman's consent. By the time it reached the floor, the bill no longer repealed abortion laws from the criminal code. In essence, it said that abortions were criminal unless they were justifiable—justifiable abortions being those performed with a woman's consent by a physician before the 24th week of pregnancy or with a woman's consent by a physician after the 24th week of pregnancy if her life was in danger. This bill vastly expanded the conditions under which a woman might legally obtain an abortion, but it did not fundamentally challenge the state's right to participate in the abortion decision or to place the preservation of fetal life after viability over the woman's right to control her own body regardless of the stage of pregnancy. It gave final authority not to women but rather to doctors and lawyers—a development lawmakers favored over pure repeal. Known as the Cook/Leichter bill, this liberal reform passed both houses of the legislature and was signed into law in 1970, making New York the nation's "abortion mill" for the next three years.

To understand the demise of the repeal campaign, it is important to know that there was an abortion rights movement which preceded and remained distinct from the women's liberation movement. This movement was made up of people who saw a bad situation and who took action to make it better, but who were not grounded in a feminist analysis identifying each woman's need to control her own body as fundamental to women's liberation. This movement included groups

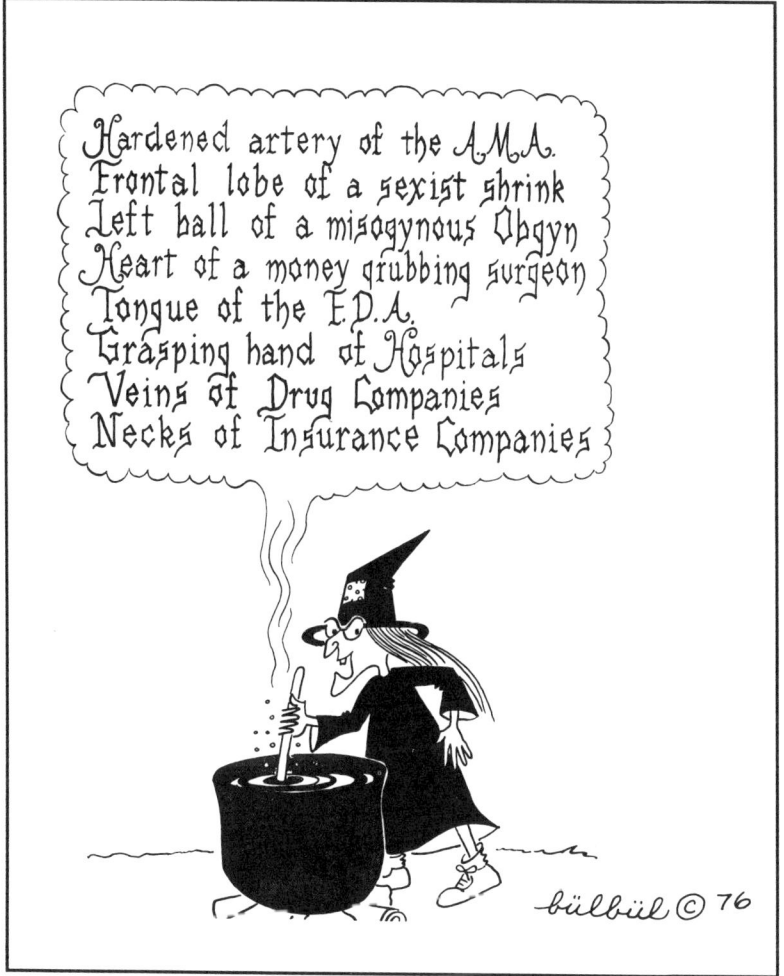

and individuals such as the Association for the Study of Abortion, which formed in 1966; legislators in New York and other states who supported ALI bills; the Rev. Howard Moody, who, with the help of Arlene Carmen, founded the Clergy Consultation Service on Abortion, and the many clergy members who followed in his footsteps by arranging underground abortions.

Other reformers include Lawrence Lader, who published a book on illegal abortion in 1966 and who publicly stated that he would not refuse referrals to women seeking abortions; Bernard Nathanson, who, along with Lader, helped found NARAL, and who worked to make legal abortions available to women in New York in the early 1970s; Bill

Baird, who began challenging archaic birth control laws in 1965; public policy, social welfare, and population control activists and organizations whose own goals would be furthered by legal abortion; and mainstream liberal political activists such as the members of the Committee for Progressive Legislation (CPL), a Schenectady-based "female voluntary association" which Lader, Cook, and the *New York Times* cite as the most influential lobby on the abortion issue.

In interviews for this project, most former CPL members made it clear that they did not see themselves as part of the feminist movement. In fact, they were offended by "women's libbers," although they appreciated that, by comparison, they appeared sedate and rational, a fact which made them especially effective as lobbyists. CPL members do not remember discussing the implications of the restrictions in the 1970 Cook/Leichter bill. If it had not been for repeal activists insisting that the bill was in fact not a repeal bill but a liberal reform bill, they would have entirely overlooked the question of whether or not this bill acknowledged a woman's right to control her own body. As it was, they issued a newsletter containing a statement that the Cook/Leichter bill *was* a repeal bill and that any claims to the contrary should be ignored.

The difference between ALI reform and pure repeal was easy for everyone to see. The ALI exceptions would not help most women, so it did not enjoy much grassroots support. Repeal, on the other hand, would allow all women to have abortions, and women worked for repeal out of self-interest. The 1970 Cook/Leichter bill also improved things for many women, so it was only those who looked beyond the immediate need for early abortion to the long-range goal of women's liberation or of libertarian government who took the position that even broad reform was incompatible with repeal. Cindy Cisler was one of those people.

When Cindy got involved in the women's liberation and abortion movements, they were both still very small. Grassroots women's liberation groups were just starting to spring up across the country. The National Organization for Women (NOW), founded in 1966, was beginning to get on its feet with a national membership under 2,000. In 1967, NOW had drafted a Bill of Rights for Women to be presented to political candidates in the 1968 elections. This Bill of Rights included "control of one's body" and called for repeal, a position which cost the organization a part of its membership when conservatives (who thought that abortion was a "women's liberation" issue more than a "women's rights" issue) left to form the Women's Equity Action League. The New York NOW chapter, although comparatively powerful and radical within the organization, was still hard for most women to find. Cindy and other women who heard rumors about women's liberation groups simply called everyone they knew to ask for information until they finally tracked down NOW-NY or New York Radical Women.

Cindy became active in both organizations. She did not come out of a New Left or Old Left (Communist) background, and she identified less with socialist-feminists and more with radical feminists like the women who would form Redstockings of Women's Liberation—the group that coined the phrases "consciousness-raising," "the personal is political," and "sisterhood is powerful." She was a close associate of Irene Peslikis, who was a founding member of Redstockings and who was very active in early abortion rights demonstrations. In an interview, Irene explained why she was drawn to women's liberation and how Redstockings formed and operated. She said:

> I had an illegal abortion at 19, and it left a very important mark on me as a young woman. It was my first realization that I was truly not an equal...
>
> When I got pregnant by accident I realized that I was very vulnerable, and that this meant a complication for my whole life for a very long time. And I was not ready for it. I was not ready to get married. I was not ready for anything like that. I was a student. I thought I was being independent by being able to have sex as a woman, but it made me realize that that wasn't a particular freedom I had as a woman. I didn't even have the right to have sex, you know? Freely. And I found myself in a position where I had to risk my life to get an abortion, and go to a place in Ohio to an unknown doctor and not tell anyone, secretly and furtively raise money, and under no anesthesia, under painful conditions, undergo an illegal abortion and then risk hemorrhaging. And it was all a dreadful experience, and an awakening to the fact that there was no escaping that I was a woman and that I had limited freedom in terms of what my rights were. I had to do all this underground, you know, it wasn't like I could get an abortion legally...It was bad enough I had to bear the burden of being the one who got pregnant, but then to have to risk my life for it was a real drag. So that really put a dent in my mind about the reality of the situation between men and women.
>
> When I heard "women's liberation" I freaked out. It was like a lightning bolt hit my head. Of course! I just kept calling places until I tracked down New York Radical Women.
>
> There was a huge anti-inaugural demonstration (in 1968) that was mainly lefty, anti-war movement people, and we asked for the right to speak in the program in the big tent at the rally. We had a really hard time and then finally after much protest they put us at the end. They put two groups, a WITCH-type (Women's International Terrorist Conspiracy from Hell) representative and a

Redstockings type. The WITCH thing was like... I think it was Marilyn Webb. She represented that group. It wasn't WITCH particularly but WITCH was affiliated with them because they had the same political outlook—that you had to demolish capitalism. We were mainly women for women, and we had to have an independent movement out of necessity. We weren't even totally convinced of the necessity of an independent movement but we had a hunch. But this convinced us, this event.

So what happened was not only did we have trouble with the men on the left but we had trouble with the WITCH contingent. We had to even surround the platform at one point for Shulie [Shulamith Firestone] to get up there and speak—we had to grip hands... Finally she got up there in spite of all the protest and everything and gave this magnificent strong feminist speech. And the men in the audience—it was really disgusting. "Take her off the stage and fuck her!" It was unbelievable. And that convinced us that there was no question about it. It was not our choosing to have an independent women's movement. We had to have it. Period.

[Redstockings] had to have a manifesto. It was a big thing to have a manifesto because one of the things we realized was that there were these important differences between groups and we had to make ourselves clear. We wanted to be a strong entity. If we kept getting diluted by other people's "capitalist" ideas we'd never get anywhere. We would never really progress and get the ideas out to women—the right ideas. And we knew that it was only the right ideas that are going to appeal to women. They aren't going to fall for this other baloney about capitalism. It wasn't true that we were oppressed because of capitalism. I mean, [capitalism] was oppressive but that wasn't the direct cause of women's oppression.

The "right ideas" came directly from women themselves through the process of consciousness-raising, the practice of speaking personally in small groups. Irene remembers doing a poster with the words "Tell It Like It Is," "Speak Pain To Recall Pain," and "Bitch Sister Bitch!" The idea was that when it came to their own experience, women were the experts.

"Women are the Experts" was the battle cry in Irene's first abortion protest. On February 13, 1969, she and other women attended a hearing on New York's proposed ALI reform bill. The "experts" on the panel were 14 men and a nun. Irene and the other women were so outraged that they stood up and demanded to be allowed to testify. When they were locked out of the hearing, they began to tell the truth about their own illegal abortions in front of national television cameras. The *Daily News* headlines read "Gals Squeal for Repeal," but the power of their action touched other women who had undergone abortions in secret.

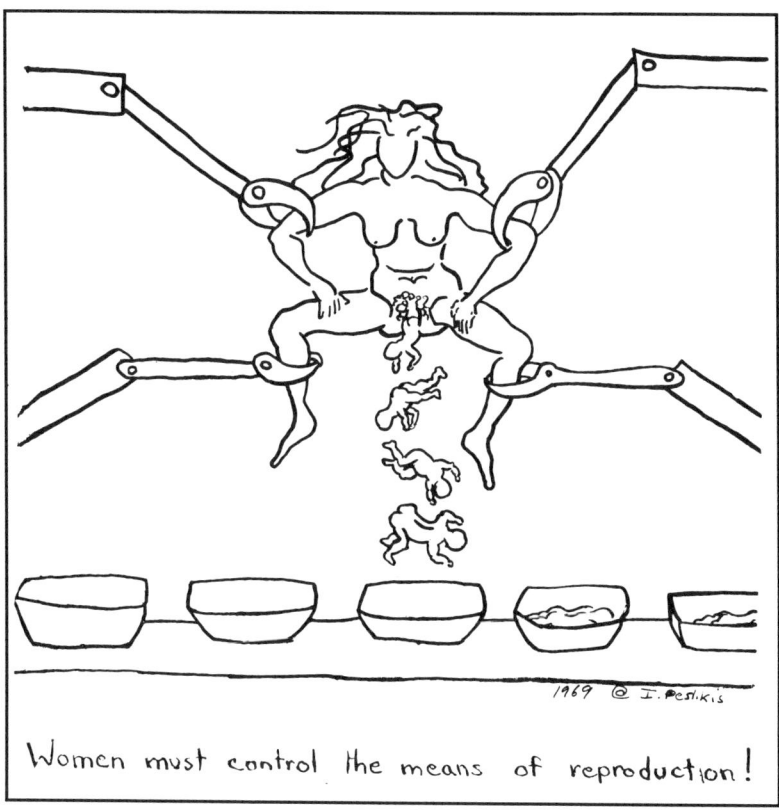

Women must control the means of reproduction!

Telling the truth about illegal abortions was an important tool in radical feminists' assault on abortion laws. Many radical feminists refused to lobby the legislature because they viewed that level of tacit agreement with the existing patriarchal power structure as inherently reformist. Legislators were invited, however, when Irene and other Redstockings organized an abortion speak-out in Washington Square Methodist Church the following month. The speak-out amounted to consciousness-raising for the public. Irene explained:

> The speak-out occurred after the abortion hearing break-up. We decided it was absolutely necessary for women to go public about what was really going on. We were getting abortions anyway. Illegally. And risking our lives and being devastated by this experience. It was just like everybody was ignoring the reality. We had to speak up for ourselves. Again, it's like, "Speak pains to recall pains," "Bitch, sisters, bitch," and "Tell it like it is!" We learned that from the Black movement, the civil rights movement. You have to defend your own rights. Nobody's going to do it for you. You have

to tell the truth about what's going on.

We got together and we decided we all had to testify about our illegal abortions. And we were going to invite all the quote "dignitaries" of the abortion movement that had existed thus far, and the press and the media. And we were all going to get up and say we had illegal abortions. Now, this was at a time when it was still illegal, so it meant you risked your job, you risked your reputation, whatever social amenities you might have—which might be negligible!—you risked them...

Redstockings organized a panel. I think it was about 15 women... We had various women who had different experiences—not hard to find, believe me!—and a church packed full of people who showed up with a vengeance. Everybody was interested in this speak-out. They had never heard of such a thing! They never believed that women would do this. Like, this is secret, right? Women do this in secret. It was like a bomb to have this speak-out because it instigated all kinds of feelings in the audience. You know, women got up and started telling about their abortions from the middle of the audience, they weren't on the panel. All of a sudden they realized that this was something that had been bothering them for the longest time, and they hadn't been able to talk about it. We released that. We freed them by doing this. And that happened in a larger sense because we got publicity. So that all these women out there knew that we had spoken out about abortion and said the truth. There were a lot of us who were telling the truth all of a sudden. It was a great thing! All of a sudden there were a whole bunch of women telling the truth about abortion. Finally! Finally! We were saying, "Yeah, we did it, we had it, and we want our rights. We want to have legal, free abortion...!"

I think that our contribution, the radical contribution, was to give a real momentous push. That's what I think we did. I don't think things would have moved like they did without that. Because it was so true and authentic and real. Everybody felt it.

At the speak-out, Cindy stood up and urged women there to tell the truth to lawmakers in Albany. She believed that women had to demand exactly what they wanted from the legislature, and in the pivotal years of 1969 and 1970 she served as a bridge between feminists and lobbyists. About her work with New Yorkers for Abortion Law Repeal (New Yorkers) she said:

> At that time Jim Clapp [Cindy's long-time partner and associate] was the president and I was the treasurer... We had started working almost full-time. He had quit his job teaching and I had taken a "temporary time out from architecture" to work full-time on this because it was in the air that things were about to change. It was

not just an illusion. It was élan that was in the air. There was a sense that people could make a difference... But in terms of New Yorkers for Abortion Law Repeal, it was the first group set up on feminist principles specifically to repeal abortion laws and not settle for reform—that's a real important part.

There had been abortion groups in many different states, mostly reform. Some were repeal groups like Pat Maginnis and Lana Phelan's group out in California. We—New Yorkers for Abortion Law Repeal—were started by New York-NOW as a way to bring lots of other people into NOW through a particular issue. Because NOW always got people in through a particular issue that they got excited about whether it was childcare or job discrimination or very much abortion at that point. That was how we did it. It was a way of funding that work, through having an umbrella group that took in all kinds of other people who didn't yet know they were feminists, or who weren't ready for feminism generally. But there were just so many doors to feminism and this was a real major one that was wide open and the winds were blowing through at a big rate. So New Yorkers got started and people from Ethical Culture and the Civil Liberties Union and the humanists and Unitarians and all kinds of people and people from all around the state joined...

At first people who were already in the abortion movement who'd worked on reform were somewhat leery to bring it up—believe it or not—as a woman's issue... They'd say, "That will scare the legislators..." But what is it, you know? It is a public health issue, it is a doctor's rights issue, it is a population control issue, it is all those other things, but finally it's this damn woman who is pregnant and who doesn't want to be pregnant and she's going to do something about it... So pretty soon it became obvious that saying, "Hey, it's the woman's right," was a very powerful, American, democratic, libertarian argument that appealed to a lot of people... The idea that it was someone's right, and that those whose right it was were going to claim it and were really going to work on it out of self-interest, like the civil rights movement and all these other very powerful movements have been built on self-interest. That was the spark that made the already existing current of older abortion reformers take light and see that there was a possibility of something they had never even dared dream about—or if they did they'd quickly draw in their horns and say, "Oh, we'll never get that far."

It was this boldness of saying, "Hey, it's my right!" plus the already existing abortion movement—as quite distinct from the feminist movement. Without both of those, nothing could have happened. Because women sitting around and talking or demonstrating or even breaking into hearings as feminists alone could not have done it, and this reform movement mousing along without an infusion of feminism couldn't have done anything much either except pass a bunch more [ALI] laws.

In 1969, when the Cook/Leichter bill consisted of a series of deletions repealing abortion laws from the criminal code, the different wings of the abortion movement were one big happy family. In 1970, when Cook changed the bill from repeal to broad reform, activists faced a difficult choice and made different decisions. The Cook bill now stipulated that only physicians could perform abortions, that the procedure could not be performed after the twenty-fourth week of pregnancy—unless the woman's life was in danger—and that informed consent would be required. NOW leaders at the national level urged continued support of the bill, and upstate New York chapters followed suit. The newly formed National Association for the Repeal of Abortion Laws disapproved of the changes but elected to back the bill anyway. New Yorkers held fast to its support for repeal and opposition to reform. Cindy and other members tried first to convince Cook to restore the bill to its original form and then to find a sponsor for a new repeal bill. Being ultimately unsuccessful in both endeavors, and with nothing left to work for, New Yorkers reluctantly began to work against the Cook/Leichter bill. Cindy said:

> We were considered just horrible people who wanted women to die. We wanted women to be left bloody and mangled on the street...We were portrayed as people who wanted everybody with a coat hanger to do an abortion, which was nuts, because that wasn't our viewpoint. [Our view] was, "Leave the door open for the world to develop as it is about to do."

One very wealthy, influential member of New Yorkers, Ruth Smith, vehemently opposed the organization's stand against reform. Charging that meetings had been packed and votes counted unfairly, she broke away and formed the Committee for the Cook/Leichter Bill to Repeal Abortion Laws—by now a contradiction in terms. The Committee for the Cook/Leichter Bill was begun with seed money from NARAL. NARAL was Lader's baby, and the moral of the story is partly that he who has access to major publishers gets to make history. In *Abortion Two,* Lader wrote:

> The extremist faction of New Yorkers for Abortion Law Repeal, headed by Cisler and Clapp...opposed the licensed physician requirement, insisting that abortion could become completely available to women only if performed by paramedicals... Holding out for all or nothing, they pushed their boycott of the Cook bill through the New Yorkers board and general membership... NARAL's executive committee now faced a torturous decision. Although most members favored paramedicals (and NARAL would back this stand

Speak Truth to Power 45

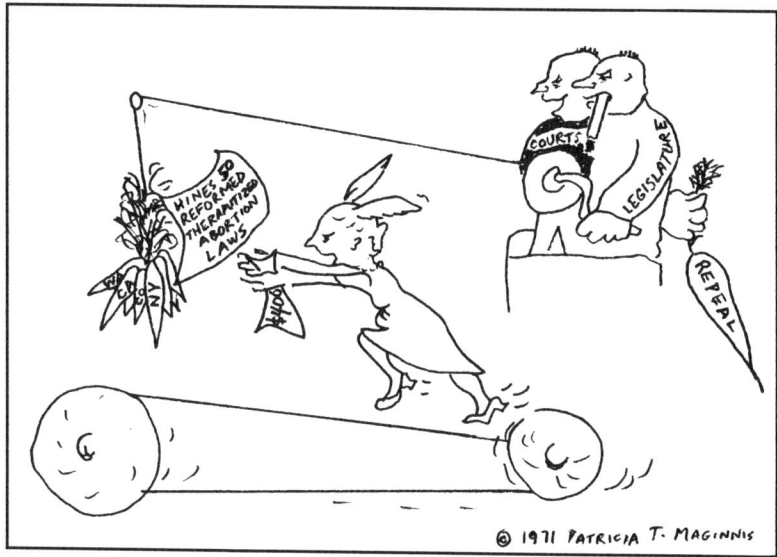

at its annual convention in the fall), we recognized that no legislature would accept paramedicals in the immediate future, and we voted to intensify our campaign for the Cook bill...[6]

Lader, virtually the only author whose writing on the New York repeal campaign has been made widely available, clearly viewed New Yorkers and other organizations intent on abolishing all abortion laws as politically naive and counterproductive. Not being grounded in a feminist or libertarian analysis which recognized the right of each woman to control her own body and therefore demanded the removal of criminal constraints in the abortion debate, he did not consider it a problem that the physician restriction rendered the Cook/Leichter bill a liberal reform. It was only in his account of the Assembly Codes Committee decision to place a 24-week time limit on abortion that he wrote that to accept such a compromise would be "the first retreat from our repeal position."[7] He concluded that the limitation "would only affect a handful of women."[8] About this "handful" Cindy said:

> After the law was changed, our group got people calling us looking for late abortions. All the abortion referrals and counseling that I did and that anyone ever did kept us going. Because it kept being individual women saying, "Things aren't working right for me..." There are those who are considered quite eminent and expert who were never seen on the issue before the late 1970s who will say, "Only two percent of women get late abortions anyway," essentially saying, "To hell with those women." Nobody who was for repeal ever said to hell with anybody. Every woman is a one hundred per cent sample of herself.

Lader stated that NARAL's decision to continue to support the bill "was a matter of weighing NARAL's philosophical stand against the reality of almost unrestricted abortion for thousands of women."[9] When, five days after the 24-week restriction was added, 2,000 people rallied in Union Square in support of repeal, Lader concluded that this was but a "flyspeck" at a time when "every organization in the movement now concentrated on a final strategy to win."[10]

Obviously, "every organization" did not concentrate on passing the Cook/Leichter bill. As Lader himself points out, some groups, most notably New Yorkers and a coalition called People to Abolish Abortion Laws, actively opposed the bill. Furthermore, it is difficult to know how many people knew exactly what they were supporting. As mentioned earlier, members of the Committee for Progressive Legislation were assured that the 1970 Cook/Leichter bill was a repeal bill and that arguments to the contrary should be ignored. Some members of New Yorkers may have been given the same misinformation. While Ruth Smith claimed that Cindy and Jim packed meetings and miscounted votes, they say that when she left to form the Committee for the Cook/Leichter Bill she took the New Yorkers mailing list. They charge that she opened mail addressed to New Yorkers, cashed the donations enclosed, and returned letters thanking contributors and activists for their contribution to the repeal of abortion laws. After the Cook/Leichter bill passed, many people seemed to think that abortion laws *had* been repealed. Cindy said:

> There was one of the usual, somewhat careless, well-meaning polls which said to a good cross-section of the public, "In New York State now any woman who wants an abortion can get one legally. What do you think about that?" Of course that wasn't true. That's what we'd been for! Oh, most people thought that was just fine—as they would have if someone maybe actually had tried to pass that!

When the campaign for repeal broke into bitterly opposed factions in 1970, Cindy wrote an article titled "Abortion Law Repeal (sort of): A Warning to Women." It was first published in *Notes From the Second Year*. Cindy explained:

> One of the few things everyone in the women's movement seems to agree on is that we have to get rid of abortion laws and make sure that any woman who wants an abortion can get one. We all recognize how basic this demand is: it sounds like a pretty clear and simple demand too—hard to achieve, of course, but obviously a fundamental right just like any other method of birth control.

But just because it sounds so simple and so obvious and is such a great point of unity, a lot of us haven't really looked below the surface of the abortion fight and seen how complicated it may be to get what we want. The most important thing feminists have done and must keep doing is to insist that the basic reason for repealing abortion laws and making abortions available is JUSTICE: women's right to abortion...

The abortion issue is one of the few issues vital to the women's movement that well-meaning people outside the movement were dealing with on an organized basis even before the new feminism began to explode a couple of years ago. Whatever we may like to think, there *is* quite definitely an abortion movement that is distinct from the feminist movement, and the good intentions of the people in it can turn out to be either a tremendous source of support for our goals or the most tragic barrier to ever achieving them... And unless well-thought-out feminism underlies the dedication of these people, they will accept all kinds of token gains from legislators and judges and the medical establishment in the name of "getting something done—NOW..."[11]

Throughout the article, Cindy argued that as long as the government maintained a voice in the abortion debate, it would use its power to chip away at each woman's right to make her own choice about abortion. Her predictions have come true with a vengeance. In the last 17 years, we have won no new abortion rights for women, and we have lost plenty. This is not surprising. Twenty years ago, the radicals in the abortion debate were the women who demanded free abortions and the repeal of all abortion laws. Since then, the abortion "radicals" have been the right-to-lifers who harass women, bomb clinics, and fight against women's rights in courts and capitals. Politics is the art of compromise. As long as the right-to-lifers demand that women give up all our options for abortion (Outlaw all abortion!) and pro-choice activists just ask to keep what women already have (Keep Abortion Safe and Legal!) then, by definition, we will lose ground every time a compromise is made. In her article, "No More Nice Girls," Brett Harvey explained the need to "reinject the abortion rights movement with the radical ideas and spirit of the early 1970s":

> In 1970 a group of New York area feminists distributed a copy of a "model abortion law": a blank piece of paper. Their position was unequivocal: a woman's right to abortion must be absolute, because her very personhood depends on her ability to control her own reproductive system. The 1973 Supreme Court decision, through ruling that abortion was a constitutional right, stopped short of endorsing the principal that the *only* person qualified to

make a decision about abortion is the woman herself. Though radical feminists warned that the limited nature of the victory made it vulnerable to erosion and even reversal, most of us assumed in 1973 that the battle was over—that our right to abortion was virtually assured.

The Cassandras were right, of course... The response of the women's movement to [the right-to-life] onslaught took a number of different forms—indeed, as many forms as there were explanations for what had gone wrong... But what was more important was that the New Right had changed the terms of the debate. Their attack on abortion rights had all the earmarks of a Holy War, because it focused on abortion as a moral issue; the fetus has a right to life which is paramount and sacred. Abortion is murder, pure and simple. In this context, it was easy to paint women who want abortions as selfish hedonists seeking pleasure without responsibility. This dovetailed neatly with a mounting unease among liberals about the evils of "self-fulfillment" and the supposed resulting disintegration of the family. Feminists and pro-abortion activists were not in a position to frame the debate in their own terms as they had in the early 1970s, but were forced into a defensive posture.

The strategy of liberal mainstream organizations like Planned Parenthood and NARAL was to focus on abortion as a personal *choice*. "Abortion is something personal. *Not* political." ran the headline in a Planned Parenthood ad in the *New York Times* on April 26, 1981. The same Sunday NARAL ran a full-page ad which bannered, "The real issue is not abortion. The issue is the right of individuals to live free of government intrusion" ... The New Right... had guilt-tripped the abortion rights movement into soft-pedaling the most radical element of the abortion issue: that women's autonomy *must* include the right to express ourselves as sexual beings. That women cannot control our own destinies unless we can control our own reproductive function.[12]

We won abortion rights in the 1970s—and we lost abortion rights in the 1980s—in part because of the radicals who defined the terms of the debate. Radicals play an extremely important role in social movements. In "The Power of History," Kathie Sarachild asserted that in the close New York State vote, some legislators testified that they voted for reform in order to accommodate women's demands enough to prevent the possibility of repeal. She wrote, "It was both because of the work of the radicals and to stop the radicals that the reform came into being."[13]

Radicals define the left border of the struggle. They enable less extreme followers to move forward into the middle ground with the contrasting appearance of reasonableness and moderation. Because the radicals exist, there exists a new middle ground in which compromises may be made. Compromises and reforms will satisfy some of the people in the movement, but, by definition, they will not satisfy the radicals who seek revolutionary change at the root of the problem. As a movement becomes popular, and therefore seemingly successful, it also moves farther away from the pioneers who provided its original spark. Their ideas become modified and watered down to a level that a broad base of followers can find acceptable. Eventually, the entire debate shifts to the right, and the pioneers and their radical visions and actions will disappear from view unless someone fights to keep their legacy alive.

In a "Letter on Movement Pioneers," published in *Feminist Revolution,* Redstockings member Patricia Mainardi explained how radical history is buried and radical leaders are made invisible. She wrote:

> The second wave is like the occupying army, not the avant garde. It can and will move only into completely cleared and risk-free territory... I keep coming back to my "cleared ground" metaphor—that being pushed off our own cleared ground means that we still have to fight to get any writing of ours published, to be able to speak in public; forget access to the media, that's been made impossible. And if the movement doesn't go forward, it will corrode, people drop away, the momentum slows down and stops, and then the gears start grinding backwards towards repression.[14]

In an interview for the "Abortion Rap" workshops, "Jane" said:

> I worry about the women's movement. I feel like the beginnings of a theory were, how shall I put this—that we turned our backs on some very important principles. One of the things that happens in our society is that good ideas get coopted. And what gets coopted is what it looks like and not what it's really about. Like the difference between providing abortions and providing a situation that tries to give control back to a person over her own life. That kind of thing. And so we have been grateful for legal battles won that certainly are not firmly planted in the ground.

The role of the radical is to know what she wants. If she doesn't know what she wants, she can't demand it. If she doesn't demand it, she won't get it. In all likelihood, she won't get it even if she does demand it. The radical will be followed by reformers who will sell her demands for fundamental change right down the river. Her job is to make that river as wide as possible so that the compromisers can at least begin their journey from a far left bank. The next chapter is written to help young activists fulfill that role.

Notes to Chapter 3

1. Kathie Sarachild, "The Power of History," ed. Redstockings of Women's Liberation, *Feminist Revolution* (New York: Random House, 1975) p. 20.

2. *Ibid.,* p. 13.

3. Bernard Nathanson with Richard Ostling, *Aborting America* (Garden City: Doubleday, 1979) p. 57.

4. *Ibid.,* pp. 32-33.

5. Press release issued by Assembly members Cook and Leichter, April 18, 1969. (Copied from Committee for Cook/Leichter Bill files donated to Senator Leichter.)

6. Lawrence Lader, *Abortion II: Making the Revolution* (Boston: Beacon Press, 1973) p. 130.

7. *Ibid.,* p. 136.

8. *Ibid.*

9. *Ibid.*

10. *Ibid.,* p. 137.

11. Cindy Cisler, "Abortion Law Repeal (sort of): A Warning to Women," eds. Anne Koedt, Ellen Levine, and Anita Rapone, *Radical Feminism* (New York: Quadrangle/The New York Times Book Co., 1970) pp. 151-163.

12. Brett Harvey, "No More Nice Girls," *Pleasure and Danger* Carole S. Vance, ed. (Boston: Routledge and Kegan Paul, 1984) pp. 204-206.

13. Sarachild, *op. cit.*, p. 22.

14. Patricia Mainardi, "Letter on Movement Pioneers," *Feminist Revolution, op. cit.*, p. 44.

Lessons for the 1990s

Twenty years ago abortion had the power to spark a social movement. It is doing the same thing today. If we understand our heritage, we will have a better chance of drawing on the strengths—and avoiding the pitfalls—of the pioneers of the abortion movement.

One of the most important things the abortion movement did for women was show them that they could take direct action on their own behalf. Women were not just victims of the problem of illegal abortion. They were also part of the solution to the problem of illegal abortion. Through working on abortion, many women learned that they could help themselves. The basic idea behind self-help is that we don't have to convince someone in authority to do something for us. We don't have to wait for permission. Sometimes we can claim the power we want by acting as if we already have it. The philosophy of self-help can be applied not only to abortion but also to other issues where the state, the "system," or "the way things are" disempowers women.

In the late 1960s and early 1970s, women worked with one another to define problems and to provide solutions. Historically, it has been through examining our own experience, providing our own analysis of oppression, and formulating our own plans for activism, that women have become empowered to work for our own liberation. This process, called "consciousness-raising," was the backbone of the women's liberation movement. Irene Peslikis of Redstockings said:

> We really knew that [consciousness-raising] was where the truth was. And it was not only where the truth was. It was the best way to organize women, because it allowed them to perceive the truth themselves about their own situation...Imagine what it was like for me to have been this closet feminist, basically, for practically my whole life, and all of a sudden to hear there's such a thing as women's liberation. Just the term turns me on. I know that's true. And then finding this group and walking into a room full of women who are just like me.

Consciousness-raising was liberating, but it and the homogeneity of the women's liberation movement were a double-edged sword. For example, middle-class white women worked primarily with other white women "just like them" to define illegal abortion as a problem. Drawing from their own experience, they analyzed abortion policy as a power issue—the power of men over women. They did not, however, always analyze it in terms of racial or class domination. Many white women were bewildered when Black militants worked against abortion law repeal or even when some Black feminists chose not to support the abortion rights movement. Long-time activist Sojourner McCauley explained:

> I think that we were all involved with [abortion rights] as women of color. But for most of us who at that time were into what we called "nation-building," it was something that was kept in the closet. It was not something that you actively went out and said, "I'm for abortion rights." Because according to the system at that point, abortion and birth control were forms of genocide for women of color. So that if you advocated for abortion, then you were part of that monster that wanted to perform genocide on the race. So you didn't say anything about it.
>
> I don't think for me it was an issue of whether I was into nation-building or not. For me, it was, "I want to have the right to make the decision if I don't want to have children anymore." If I decide that I want to take birth control, I want the right to be there to be able to do that. And I'm real clear on that, okay? It's like, a lot of us who are women of color—I know I would not have an abortion, but that does not mean I will not fight like hell for all women to have that right. It's my choice not to have one, but I think that everyone should have the choice.
>
> I think that for a lot of women, especially when we are talking about women of color versus women of non-color or women of resources, women of resources or women of non-color are always going to be able to have abortions, okay? Because they have access. As women of color, we don't have that access. Because we don't have the money, we don't have the whatever. If you take away our right to legal abortion you have closed us into a closet. Taking the right away from women really is not taking it from all women. It's taking it from a certain class of women, certain colors of women...
>
> In order for any social change to happen, you have to do coalition-building. You have to get a broad base...Back in the '60s when NOW was first coming into power, they were not inclusive. They were not inclusive of women of color. They were not inclusive of differently-abled women. They were not inclusive of a lot of folks. And as a result they have a very bad reputation within my community as a woman of color, and in other communities. Because they did not address the issues that we had. They *now* want

to do coalition-building around abortion rights. And to be quite honest, a lot of us don't trust them. You cannot coalition build without a level of trust...

One of the most exciting things about the current movement for reproductive freedom is the sense that it will be more inclusive than the early pro-abortion movement and the recent pro-choice movement. On April 7 and 8, 1989, the Women of Color Partnership of the Religious Coalition for Abortion Rights and the American Civil Liberties Union Reproductive Freedom Project cosponsored a conference called "In Defense of Roe." Women from diverse ethnic and organizational backgrounds came together to discuss a new women-of-color agenda for the reproductive rights movement. To address the lack of trust that has existed, and to lay the foundation for respectful working relationships in the future, women presented a statement at the close of the conference. It read:

> There is a real need recognized by the people at this conference, and to some extent by the mainstream pro-choice organizations, to broaden the pro-choice constituency. As part of the effort to broaden the base, women of color have been asked to support pro-choice activities...Women of color, though they have given their support, have done so with mixed emotions, because they feel quite often that they are being used, not really incorporated in the defining, articulating, and decision-making mechanisms of those organizations. To put a stop to the continuation of these practices, we will set forth a set of criteria for your consideration in order to have our participation in future activities. These include: 1) Having been empowered and considered in framing the issues and in setting the agenda, in determining activities, and in implementing activities—not only called upon to participate at the implementation stage. 2) Endorsing and supporting only those organizations that have women of color represented adequately on their boards and staffs—and that is for *us* to determine. 3) Supporting those organizations that support women of color in their programs. In addition to these criteria, to truly incorporate women of color in the mainstream, *or else call for a separate organization of women of color concerned with reproductive rights...* Until we focus on quality of life, quality of care, survival, and access issues, women of color will not automatically endorse organizations or actions. This is the context within which we will work on any issue of women's reproductive health and freedom such as access to abortion and health care, publicly funded abortion, services within and controlled by our community, forced sterilization, access to reproductive technologies that deal with infertility, infant mortality, pre-natal health, HIV testing, and forced caesarean sections. *To implement these goals we want a network of existing women-of-color organi-*

zations to set an agenda based on these priorities. Working on quality of life issues for women of color will be the vehicle for changing existing power relations... The analysis needs to always be done around the sisters who are forced to function on the bottom of this society, the sisters who have the lowest income, who have the least access to services who have the hardest time. That's who we need to hear from. What does reproductive rights mean to you?

There is not yet a formal, autonomous, women-of-color network to join or support, but activists who want to support reproductive freedom in a holistic, revolutionary context can do so in a number of ways. If you live in an ethnically diverse part of the country and are active in predominantly white pro-choice and women's groups, you can push for significant woman-of-color representation on your boards and you

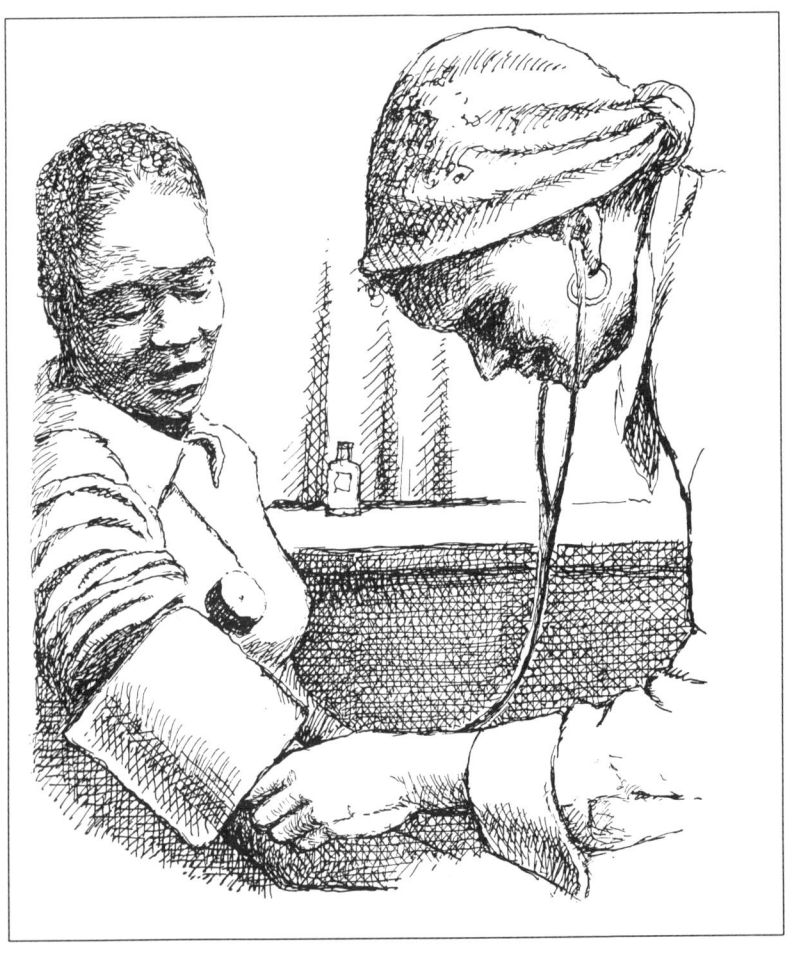

can attend board meetings to make sure that they are not simply "colorized" but in fact respond to what women of color bring to the movement. You can, for example, see that such organizations' mission statements are re-evaluated and expanded where necessary. You can also try to be sure that, where possible, such organizations give genuine support in the form of publicity, volunteers, and money to programs and events sponsored by predominantly women-of-color organizations working on a broad range of reproductive freedom issues. Or, as an individual, you can choose to withdraw your support from narrow organizations and decide instead to give your time and/or money to more inclusive groups. If you are starting a new group, you can make racial and cultural diversity an explicit part of your membership structure, limiting the participation of white women if necessary. To find out what women-of-color organizations are already active in your area, you can contact the Women of Color Partnership of the Religious Coalition for Abortion Rights or the National Black Women's Health Project, both of which are listed in the back of this pamphlet.

If you are a white woman and you live in a part of the country that is predominantly white, you can still work on any number of reproductive freedom issues including medicaid coverage, low-cost childcare, lesbian rights, rape and sexual assault, and sex education, to name a few. In any part of the country, you can start white women's anti-racism groups in new or existing organizations. Or you can follow the advice of Byllye Avery, Director of the National Black Women's Health Project. At the conference "In Defense of Roe," she explained:

> What I got to say to my white sisters—because you got to start doing this—you have got to start working down your color line. You have got to—I don't mean on the surface—you have got to go in, find poor white women, and you have got to start working with them. Because that is the only way you are going to get the correct analysis that will give you the same perspective from which we all can work. And it will make you a better worker when you come to work with us.

No matter how you decide to work, you need to be aware of the dangers of single-issue organizing. When "single-issue" organizing means that an organization's mission statement addresses *only* abortion and that it will not endorse (much less actively support) related reproductive and sexual issues, or when it means that diverse groups are expected to work together without genuinely respecting diverse concerns, this strategy misses the boat in a big way. At its most limiting, single-issue organizing means working with anyone who will agree on your issue, no matter how racist or classist their strange-bedfellow motives may be. It means not wearing your politics on your sleeve, not offending your most wealthy or "respectable" supporters, not telling the truth about what you really want if it doesn't fit the party line. Most importantly, it means not connecting abortion to other reproductive control issues, not giving yourself the opportunity to learn from and be strengthened by women who are working on equally vital related issues, and not working on those issues yourself. In an interview for this project, Brenda Joyner, Director of the Tallahassee Women's Health Center, explained:

> We have been so single issue that what we have done in effect is to eliminate this whole issue of choice—even though we call it a choice movement. It has alienated many of the very women who we say are critical to our success, such as Black women, for example, and Black leadership within the Black community...
> In this country right now, most women who are on medicaid cannot obtain an abortion, because the government has withdrawn support from those women. They are basically saying that those women who want abortions and who are under the medicaid program do not have the same rights as women who are on medicaid and who want to carry their pregnancy to term. What position does that put these women in? They are either forced to carry a pregnancy which they cannot afford in economic or emotional terms, or they are forced to look into other options for controlling their reproductive lives, such as sterilization. The government will not pay for a $200 or $300 abortion procedure for a poor woman on medicaid. But it will pay for a $2,000 to $3,000 sterilization procedure for that same poor woman. So women are basically being coerced either into having children they cannot afford or do not want, or they are being coerced into "choosing" sterilization where there is no choice.

The language of "choice" has become problematic over the last two decades. On the one hand, it has been used by liberals as a euphemism for "the A word" (as in, "I'm not in favor of abortion, I'm in favor of choice!") On the other hand, these same liberals have avoided discussion of any choices other than abortion. Historically, white, heterosexual, able-bodied, middle-class men and women in the population control, birth control, eugenics, and abortion rights movements have not respected the choices of people who were different from them. Byllye Avery explained:

> We need to first understand the meaning of the word "respect"—for ourselves; and respect for others, wherever they are. People are

here because we are working for the same cause. It doesn't mean that everybody has to be in the same place. Let me say to you, coalition-building goes along a continuum. And we will have to have people who are all places along that continuum. Not everybody will be "here." But neither will everybody be "there." What we have to do group-wise, organization-wise, is the same thing we have to do individually. You may meet a woman who might say to you, "I personally can't have an abortion." And she might be having baby number 31. And you can believe that that woman really needs to have an abortion rather than having baby number 31. But what you need to do for her is respect her choice to have baby number 31. And by respecting her choice to have baby number 31, she can support you around your abortion decision. That's what the crux of it is about.

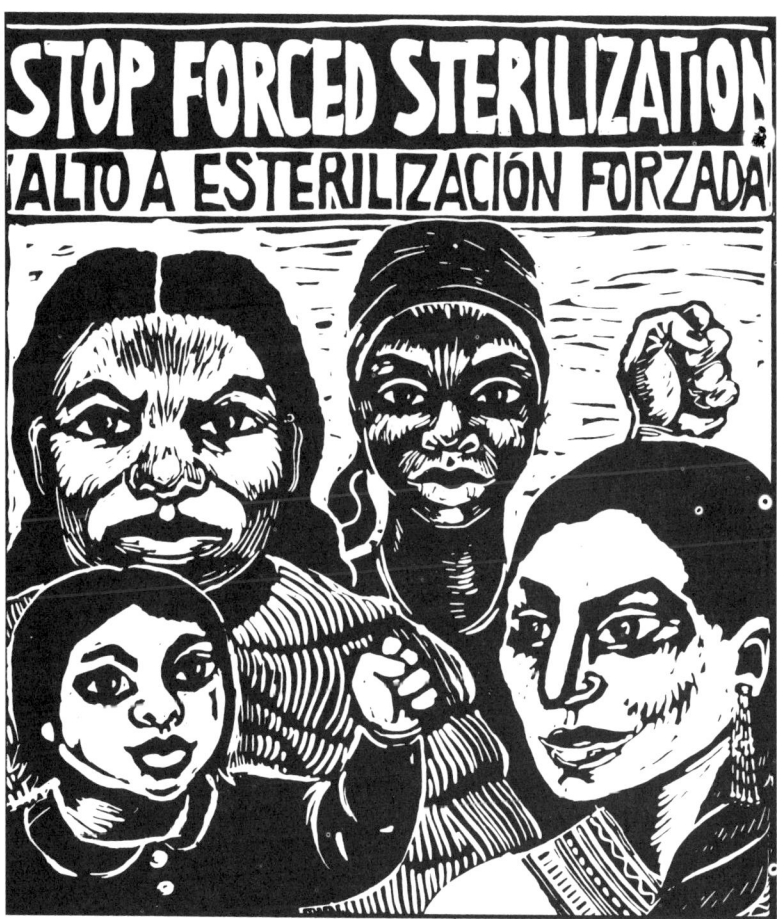

The biggest challenge that we face is learning to build coalitions with people who may be different from us. In an interview for this project, Sojourner McCauley explained:

> In terms of coalition-building, there are several things that we need to be real cognizant about. One is that when you have a coalition, you have different groups that are working on the same issue on a broad base. So that in essence the coalition members must trust each other. If there is no trust factor then the coalition-building will not work...
> A lot of organizations have problems with other organizations that they have never worked out. They need to work them out. They need to put the issues on the table and talk about the internal whatever. If I find that this organization is racist and I need them on a coalition because they have either money, numbers, and/or both, then I need to talk about their racism. We need to sit and talk about—how we are going to deal with the fact that, within some organizations, as "politically correct" as they may be, they may be oppressive to other groups. How do you deal with a group that does not bring up the issue of women of color? How do you deal with a group that doesn't deal with the issue of poor women? And how do you tell them, "These are the issues that we have with you? You have numbers. We need to be fighting on this main issue—abortion rights—together. But we also need to talk about what's happening down here, so that we don't build a bridge on sand. It will collapse when the numbers get on the bridge." We have been able to form these large coalitions, [but] there's been no foundation for the coalitions. And then when you look, the coalition has fallen into the river with all the people drowning. That makes no sense to me. If we take the time to make a concrete foundation for this coalition to be built on, then when we get the coalition running, it will stay in place forever.

Gaining trust and building coalitions means working at a grassroots level. Many organizations that call themselves grassroots organizations are in fact really just membership organizations. They depend on member dollars and volunteer labor to survive, but policy is set at the top. Volunteer empowerment does not mean encouraging a woman to think for herself about what she wants or supporting her in her efforts to get it; it means having her do more and more of the work to carry out the policies that the board and staff have already set. There are plenty of women who have lots of energy for grassroots activism, but very often their ideas are not supported because they don't bring money or volunteers into existing organizations. There are also plenty of women who are poor or of color or who for various reasons might support abortion

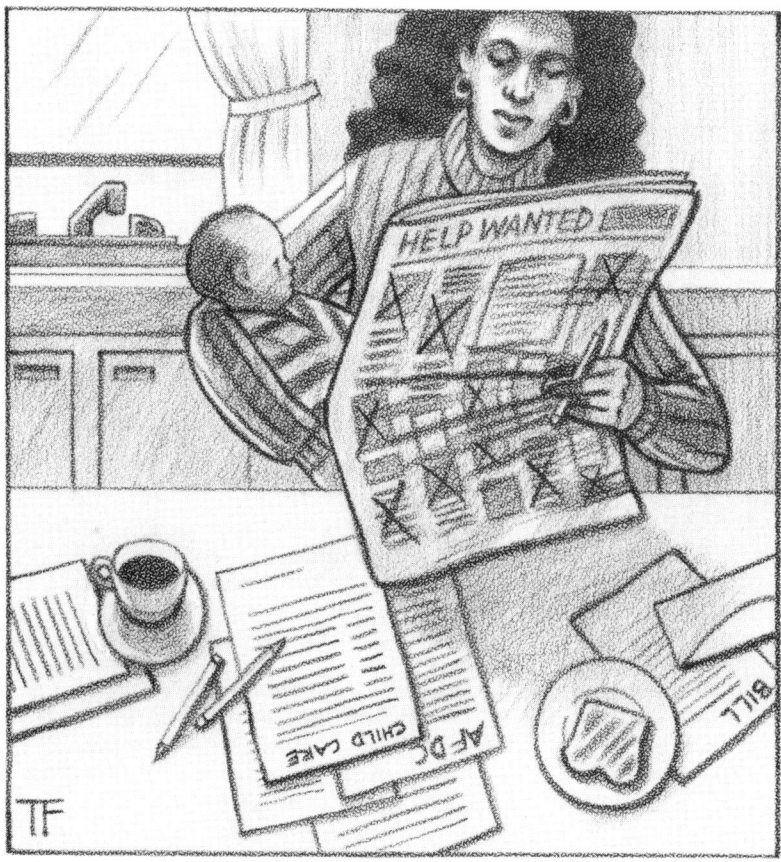

rights but who find that just keeping abortion "safe and legal" is not on their top five list of reproductive freedom issues. One way to gain trust and understanding is to really listen to what other people identify as the problems facing them and to respect their need to work on those immediate issues first. Sojourner McCauley explained:

> Back in the '60s when the Black Panthers did their Breakfast Program, people connected to the Panthers not because they picked up guns and said they believed in armed struggle. They picked up on the Black Panthers because they fed their kids...A lot of the organizing techniques that they used back then had nothing to do with the gun or robbing a bank or political change. The community knew them as the people who came and got their kids each morning to eat breakfast. The community knew them as the folks who said, "You don't have a quarter for the paper? Here's the paper, 'cause we understand the economics of this country." The community knew them as folks who came in and talked with them

about how you change shit in the schools. And how you have the right to bear arms, and what that means, you know? And if you feel it's necessary, then you should go ahead and do that—and let's talk about how this has been done in other countries. So it started from, "Let's feed the masses," to "Let's change the environment that the masses live in." People are not using these techniques anymore...I think that's what we are losing in terms of our organizing right now. We've gotten away from the very basic things that we need to do to draw masses of people together.

At the conference "In Defense of Roe," Byllye Avery expanded on this idea to show how it could be used in the reproductive rights movement. She said:

> We don't have to have everybody over here always crystal clear and pure on everything. Like, who is pure on everything? We're building coalitions here. And we are gonna have to work for issues that will lead to the end goal. [We might] work with groups that you might wonder how they are going to get there. Some groups, we'll have to organize them around health care in general—and then move them on. Some groups, we'll have to organize around sex education, sex information—and move them on. But at least you have a place to begin a dialogue. There's a whole lot of people out there that nobody is talking to. And they don't know what to do. They're turned off with these crazy [right-to-life] people. But are we talking to them? We're waiting on the very pure, and I'm saying to you, we can't do that. We have to have respect for where we are.

The last chapter of this pamphlet is designed to help you figure out where you are, where you want to go, and how you are going to get there.

5

Organizing for the Future

The "Abortion Rap" workshops use history to encourage reproductive freedom activists to envision what they really want, and to empower them to take action to get it. If you would like to do your own workshop, you might find some of these suggestions useful.

First, group members will need to arrive at a common starting point. If the group is small and the participants don't know one another, you will probably want to have a "go around" so that each woman can introduce herself, explain what her interests are, and indicate what she hopes to get out of the meeting. If the group is very big, you—or whoever is facilitating—will need to get things started. To help promote the idea that it is *your right* to envision what you *really* want, I suggest starting by showing the film "With a Vengeance" (See Resources). "With a Vengeance" is based on the "Abortion Rap" workshops and is ideally suited to this purpose. If you decide not to show the film, you might want to read a short section from this pamphlet that grabs you. Or you can simply spend more time talking about what is going on in your community, how it makes you feel, and why you have come to this meeting. One way or another, you will need to set up some kind of orientation.

When I do workshops, I like to spend some time hearing from each woman who wants to speak about all the ways that the right to control her own body is not respected. This can be a good time to share abortion stories, but I also encourage women to talk about rape, incest, street harassment, birth control, treatment from doctors, forced abortion, childcare... whatever. If you use a blackboard or a large piece of paper taped to the wall and a bunch of magic markers, and you make a laundry list of all the things women talk about, you will begin to locate abortion rights within the larger context of each woman's right to control her own body and her own life. This is the meaning of reproductive freedom.

Next, I like to spend some time brainstorming about what each woman wants abortion policy—and the abortion experience—to be. This is where your mind-expanding introduction will come in handy. Most of us have never been asked—even by pro-choice organizations—

what we really want. If group members seem stuck or stop at saying they want to "keep abortion safe and legal," you might want to ask something like, "In the best of all possible worlds..."

> Do you want to have to pay for an abortion, or do you want it to be free?
>
> Do you want to have to go to a doctor to get an abortion, or would you like to have the option of having your abortion done by a midwife or trained lay-practitioner with good medical back-up?
>
> Do you want to have to travel to get your abortion, or would you like to have someone do your abortion in your own home?
>
> Do you want the government to be the body that decides about abortion, or do you want lawmakers to be silent on the subject of what you do with your own body?

At this point, women usually begin to come up with ideas for taking action. I try to encourage women not to censor their ideas, and I generally learn something as a result. Whether women talk about planning lobbying tactics, learning to perform abortions themselves, or smuggling abortifacients like RU486 into this country, this is one of the most valuable sections of every workshop. It will help you see what other women are ready to take on and who you really want to work with.

Once you make a laundry list of all the things you *could* do, it's a good idea to share what you *are* doing, both for abortion rights and for other related causes. When you are again grounded in the reality of what's going on right now, you need to bring the meeting to a close by deciding if and how you will proceed from here. Perhaps all of you will agree on one plan of action. Perhaps you will set a time for another meeting. Perhaps a few of you will recognize an affinity and make arrangements to get together on your own. Perhaps you will decide not to form a new reproductive rights group until you have done a lot of groundwork in anti-racism. Whatever you decide, you are limited only by your imagination.

RESOURCES

- **Films and Videos**

"With a Vengeance," available from Women Make Movies, 225 Lafayette St., New York, NY, 10012, (212) 925-0606.

"La Operación," available from The Cinema Guild, 1697 Broadway, #802, New York, NY, 10019, (212) 246-5522.

"Abortion Stories North and South," available from The National Film Board of Canada, 1251 Ave. of the Americas, 16th Floor, New York, NY, 10020, (212) 586-5131.

"In Denfese of Roe," available from ACLU Reproductive Freedom Project, 132 West 43rd St., New York, NY, 10036, (212) 944-9800.

"No Going Back," available from the Federation of Feminist Women's Health Centers, 1043 University Ave., #169, San Diego, CA 92103, (619) 298-0967.

- **Organizations**

Please note: This is *not* a comprehensive list of reproductive freedom organizations. This list is intended *only* to give you a place to start your search for resources and referrals that can help you join or create the organization most suited to your needs.

Civil Rights/Abortion Rights Resources

Women of Color Partnership
Religious Coalition
for Abortion Rights
100 Maryland Ave. NE
Washington, DC 20002
(202) 543-7032

Reproductive Freedom Project
American Civil Liberties Union
132 W. 43rd St.
New York, NY 10003
(212) 944-9800

Center for Constitutional Rights
666 Broadway
New York, NY 10012
(212) 614-6464

Abortion Rights in Puerto Rico
Apartado 2172
Estacion Hato Rey
Hato Rey, Puerto Rico 00919

Health Organizations

Federation of Feminist Women's Health Centers
6221 Wilshire Blvd., Suite 419
Los Angeles, CA, 90048
(213) 930-2512

National Latina Health Organization
P.O. Box 7567
1900 Fruitvale Ave.
Oakland, CA 94601
(415) 534-1362

National Black Women's Health Project
1237 Gordon St. SW
Atlanta, GA 30310
(404) 753-0916

Hispanic Health Council
90 Cedar St., #3A
Hartford, CT 06106
(203) 527-0856

Feminist Health Center
505 W. Georgia
Tallahassee, FL 32304
(909) 224-9600

Boston Women's Health Book Collective
248 Elm St.
Somerville, MA 02144
(617) 625-0271

National Women's Health Network
1325 G St., NW
Washington, DC, 20005
(202) 347-1140

Native American Women's Health Education Resource Center
P.O. Box 572
Lake Andes, SD 57356
(605) 487-7072

Women of All Red Nations
3255 Hennepin Street
Minneapolis, MN 55408
(612) 827-5364

Activist Networks

Students Organizing Students
1601 Connecticut Ave. NW
Washington, DC 20009
(202) 822-7848

Women's Action Committee
ACT-UP
496-A Hudson St., #G4
New York, NY 10014
(212) 989-1114

"Ladies Against Women" Street Theater
Plutonium Players
1600 Woolsey, #7
Berkeley, CA 94703
(415) 841-6500

Reproductive Rights Network
(Boston R2N2)
P.O. Box 686
Jamaica Plain, MA 02130

Sexuality

Blacks Educating Blacks About Sexual Health (BEBASHI)
1528 Walnut St.
Philadelphia, PA 19102
(215) 546-4140

Eve's Garden
119 W. 57th St.
New York, NY 10019
(212) 757-8651

National Gay and Lesbian Task Force
1517 U Street, NW
Washington, DC 20009
(202) 332-6483

BIBLIOGRAPHY

Abortion is not a single issue. The history of the abortion movement cannot be understood apart from the history of connected issues including population control, women's sexuality, women's health care, and feminist theory. This bibliography is arranged by category to provide basic information on these issues as well as on the abortion movement itself.

• History of the Abortion Movement

Carmen, Arlene, and Howard Moody, *Abortion Counseling and Social Change: From Illegal Act to Medical Practice—The Story of the Clergy Consultation Service on Abortion* (Valley Forge: Judson Press, 1973).

Cisler, Lucinda, "Abortion Law Repeal (Sort Of): A Warning to Women," in *Radical Feminism,* Anne Koedt, Ellen Levine, Anita Rapone, eds. (New York: Quadrangle, 1970).

Clapp, James, "Abortion Legislation in New York: What Really Happened," in *The ZPG National Reporter* (August 1970).

Elze, Diane, "Underground Abortion Remembered," *Sojourner,* April and May, 1988 (two-part interview with JANE members).

Gordon, Linda, *Woman's Body, Woman's Right: A Social History of Birth Control in America* (New York: Penguin Books, 1974).

Harvey, Brett, "No More Nice Girls," in *Pleasure and Danger,* Carole S. Vance, ed. (Boston: Routledge and Kegan Paul, 1984).

Lader, Lawrence, *Abortion II: Making the Revolution* (New York: Beacon Press, 1973).

Lader, Lawrence, *Abortion* (New York: Bobbs-Merrill, 1966).

Maginnis, Patricia, and Lana Clarke Phelan, *The Abortion Handbook* (North Hollywood: Contact Books, 1969).

Nathanson, Bernard, *Aborting America* (Garden City: Doubleday, 1979).

Schulder, Diane, and Florynce Kennedy, *Abortion Rap* (New York: McGraw Hill, 1971).

Smith-Rosenberg, Carol, "The Abortion Movement and the AMA, 1850-1880," in *Disorderly Conduct: Visions of Gender in Victorian America* (New York: Oxford University Press, 1985).

• History of U.S. Abortion Policy

Davis, Nanette, *From Crime to Choice* (Westport: Greenwood Press, 1985).

Luker, Kristin, *Abortion and the Politics of Motherhood* (Berkeley: University of California Press, 1984).

Mohr, James, *Abortion in America: The Origins and Evolution of National Policy* (New York: Oxford University Press, 1978).

Petchesky, Rosalind, *Abortion and Women's Choice* (New York: Longman Press, 1984; Boston: Northeastern University Press, 1989).

• Women's Health Care

Arditti, Rita, Renate Duelli Klein, and Shelley Minden, *Test Tube Women* (Boston: Pandora Press, 1984).

Boston Women's Health Book Collective, eds., *Our Bodies, Ourselves,* (Boston: New England Free Press, 1970; New York: Simon and Schuster, 1979).

CARASA, Susan Davis, ed., *Women Under Attack: Victories, Backlash, and the Fight for Reproductive Freedom* (Boston: South End Press, 1989).

Corea, Gena, *The Hidden Malpractice: How American Medicine Treats Women* (New York: Harper and Row, 1985).

Ehrenreich, Barbara, and Deirdre English, *Witches, Midwives, and Nurses: A History of Women Healers* (New York: The Feminist Press, 1973).

Ehrenreich, Barbara, and Deirdre English, *Complaints and Disorders: The Sexual Politics of Sickness* (New York: The Feminist Press, 1973).

Federation of Feminist Women's Health Centers, eds., *How to Stay Out of the Gynecologist's Office* (Peace Press, 1981), available from the Federation of Feminist Women's Health Centers, see Resources.

Federation of Feminist Women's Health Centers, eds., *A New View of a Woman's Body* (New York: Simon and Schuster, 1979), available from the Federation of Feminist Women's Health Centers, see Resources.

Frankfort, Ellen, *Vaginal Politics* (New York: Quadrangle, 1972).

Gage, Suzanne, *When Birth Control Fails* (Speculum Press, 1979), available from the Federation of Feminist Women's Health Centers, see Resources.

National Women's Health Network, "Abortion Then and Now, Creative Responses to Restricted Access" (1989), a series of articles available from the Network, 1325 G Street, NW, Washington, DC 20005.

Ruzek, Sheryl Burt, *The Women's Health Movement: Feminist Alternatives to Medical Control* (New York: Praeger, 1979).

Sidel, Victor, and Ruth Sidel, eds., *Reforming Medicine: Lessons of the Last Quarter Century* (New York: Pantheon, 1984).

• Women's Sexuality

Snitow, Ann, Christine Stansell, and Sharon Thompson, eds., *Powers of Desire: The Politics of Sexuality* (New York: Monthly Review Press, 1983).

Vance, Carole S., ed., *Pleasure and Danger: Exploring Female Sexuality* (Boston: Routledge and Kegan Paul, 1984).

• Women's Liberation

de Beauvoir, Simone, *The Second Sex* (New York: Knopf, 1952).

Davis, Angela, *Women, Race and Class* (New York: Random House, 1981).

Evans, Sara, *Personal Politics: The Roots of Women's Liberation in the Civil Rights Movement & the New Left* (New York: Vintage Books, 1980).

Firestone, Shulamith, *The Dialectic of Sex: The Case for Feminist Revolution* (New York: William Morrow, 1970).

Freeman, Jo, *The Politics of Women's Liberation* (New York: Longman, 1975).

Friedan, Betty, *The Feminine Mystique* (New York: Norton, 1963).

Gornick, Vivian, and Barbara K. Moran, *Woman in Sexist Society: Studies in Power and Powerlessness* (New York: Signet, 1971).

Hole, Judith, and Ellen Levine, *Rebirth of Feminism* (New York: Quadrangle, 1971).

hooks, bell, *Feminist Theory: From Margin to Center* (Boston: South End Press, 1984).

Koedt, Anne, Ellen Levine, and Anita Rapone, eds., *Radical Feminism* (New York: Quadrangle, 1973).

Millett, Kate, *Sexual Politics* (New York: Avon, 1971).

Morgan, Robin, ed., *Sisterhood Is Powerful: An Anthology of Writings From the Women's Liberation Movement* (New York: Random House, 1970).

New York Radical Women, *Notes From the First Year (1968), Notes From the Second Year (1969), and Notes From the Third Year (1970)*, available in the Herstory Microfilm Collection, Laura X, ed., (Berkeley: Women's History Research Project, 1976).

Redstockings of Women's Liberation, eds., *Feminist Revolution* (New York: Random House, 1975), available from Archives Distribution Project, P.O. Box 2625, Gainsville, FL 32602.

• Population Control

Frankfort, Ellen, *Rosie: The Investigation of a Wrongful Death* (New York: Dial, 1978).

Hartman, Betsy, *Reproductive Rights and Wrongs: The Global Politics of Population Control and Contraceptive Choice* (New York: Harper and Row, 1987).

Littlewood, Thomas, *The Politics of Population Control* (South Bend: University of Notre Dame Press, 1975).

Shapiro, Thomas, *Population Control Politics: Women, Sterilization, and Reproductive Choice* (Philadelphia: Temple University Press, 1985).

Weisbord, Robert, *Genocide? Birth Control and the Black American* (Westport: Greenwood Press, 1975).

About South End Press

South End Press is a nonprofit, collectively run book publisher with over 150 titles in print. Since our founding in 1977, we have tried to meet the needs of readers who are exploring, or are already committed to, the politics of radical social change.

Our goal is to publish books that encourage critical thinking and constructive action on the key political, cultural, social, economic, and ecological issues shaping life in the United States and in the world. In this way, we hope to give expression to a wide diversity of democratic social movements and to provide an alternative to the products of corporate publishing.

If you would like a free catalog of South End Press books or information about our membership program—which offers two free books and a 40% discount on all titles—please write us at South End Press, 116 Saint Botolph Street, Boston, MA 02115.

Other titles of interest from South End Press:

From Abortion to Reproductive Freedom:
Transforming a Movement
Marlene Gerber Fried

Women, AIDS and Activism
ACT UP/NY Women and AIDS Handbook Group

Women Under Attack:
Victories, Backlash, and the Fight for Reproductive Freedom
Committee for Abortion Rights and Against Sterilization Abuse (CARASA)

Not An Easy Choice:
A Feminist Re-examines Abortion
Kathleen McDonnell